SPECIAL
Ops
CHURCH

DR. BILL PETERS

SPECIAL OPS CHURCH by Dr. Bill Peters
Published by Creation House
A Strang Company
600 Rinehart Road
Lake Mary, Florida 32746
www.creationhouse.com

This book or parts thereof may not be reproduced in any form, stored in a retrieval system, or transmitted in any form by any means— electronic, mechanical, photocopy, recording, or otherwise—without prior written permission of the publisher, except as provided by United States of America copyright law.

Unless otherwise noted, all Scripture quotations are from the King James Version of the Bible.

Scripture quotations marked AMP are from the Amplified Bible. Old Testament copyright © 1965, 1987 by the Zondervan Corporation. The Amplified New Testament copyright © 1954, 1958, 1987 by the Lockman Foundation. Used by permission.

Scripture quotations marked NIV are from the Holy Bible, New International Version of the Bible. Copyright © 1973, 1978, 1984, International Bible Society. Used by permission.

Design Director: Bill Johnson
Cover design by Amanda Potter

Copyright © 2008 by Dr. Bill Peters
All rights reserved

Library of Congress Control Number: 2008936179
International Standard Book Number: 978-1-59979-488-4

First Edition

08 09 10 11 12 — 9 8 7 6 5 4 3 2 1
Printed in the United States of America

This book is dedicated to my wife of thirty-eight years, Barbara L. Peters, a true special ops woman. Her honor, courage, and commitment in taking the gospel to the nations have often been above and beyond the call of duty. Her sacrifices in planting special ops churches worldwide have not gone unnoticed in heaven.

CONTENTS

Preface vii

Introduction 1

1 Defining *Special Ops* 7

2 Special Ops Church 13

3 Mission, Vision, and Guiding Principles 33

4 Unity of Command 49

5 The Objective 67

6 The Three-Phase Offensive 83

7 Security, Surprise, Simplicity 99

8 The Weapon of Choice 113

9 The Special Ops Woman 125

Notes 131

To Contact the Author 134

PREFACE

A FTER THE BIRTH of my two sons, Tony and Paul, in the 1970s, the Lord began to speak to me about their generation and the one following it. The birth of my grandson Jacob in 2006 accentuated my perception of the Lord's interest in these two emerging generations. For the first time since my grandfather Antonio Peters came to America around 1906, the Peters family had three living generations of men to whom God could release a strong generational blessing.

The willingness of the older generation to serve younger generations and the willingness of the younger generations to embrace the wisdom of seasoned saints is invaluable. This relationship of the younger and the older working together to fulfill the Great Commission and usher in the kingdom of God is priceless. Surely it fulfills the biblical model of building a holy nation, as seen in the Old Testament characters Abraham, Isaac, and Jacob. We wish our children and grandchildren great success in their radical pursuit of seeing the earth filled with the glory of the kingdom of God.

My wife Barbara and I were swept into our salvation experience through Jesus Christ during the Jesus movement in 1971. Ten million souls were saved in that movement, but statistics tell us that only about one million walk with Jesus today. In a natural war this would have been considered a terrible attrition rate. Nine million casualties out of a ten million new recruits is an unsatisfactory percentage of killed, wounded, or captured members for any army in the history of warfare. I propose that the body of Christ must do better in training the new recruits of this generation to survive the battle before them. It is my hope that this book, *Special Ops Church*, will impart the principles, tactics, and strategies of war in a way that they can be grasped and applied to the battle that lies ahead for the next generation of Christians.

I also want to thank my ministry board members, Vincent Carella and Lois Soto, for their Joshua-Caleb leadership and for lending their gifts to help establish two new generations in the faith. They, along with many others, recognize a new church paradigm under development, called the special ops church.

INTRODUCTION

T HIS BOOK, WHICH has numerous accounts of real combat experiences and analogies that bear relevance to spiritual warfare, will seem like a parable to some readers. It's written primarily to an emerging generation of believers I call special ops Christians. These bold new combatants, along with others whose leadership reflects Old Testament characters such as Joshua and Caleb, are creating a new paradigm called the special ops church. This group of youthful and senior Christians responds more to the message of the kingdom of God than to the spirit of religion. They see the church as part of the kingdom of God, but not the kingdom itself.

What is the kingdom of God? This outer working of the redemptive rule of God is best summed up in the following scriptures, which suggest that the war has been won in Christ but there remains a battle or cleanup action with enemy forces that are still active. God won the war with Satan over heaven and Earth through the death, burial, and resurrection of Jesus Christ.

> The LORD (God) says to my Lord (the Messiah), Sit at My right hand, until I make Your adversaries Your footstool.
> —PSALM 110:1, AMP

This scripture, which strongly infers that God is still engaged in battle with the Messiah's adversaries is also referred to in Matthew 26:64, Acts 2:34, 1 Corinthians 15:25, and Hebrews 12:2.

The apostle Paul explains the cleanup action this way:

> For [Christ] must be King and reign until He has put all [His] enemies under His feet. The last enemy to be subdued and abolished is death. For He [the Father] has put all things

in subjection under His [Christ's] feet. But when it says, All things are put in subjection [under him], it is evident that He [Himself] is excepted Who does the subjecting of all things to Him.

—1 CORINTHIANS 15:25–27, AMP

According to Carl von Clausewitz in his book *On War,* war is an act of violence intended to compel our opponent to fulfill our will.[1] Jesus taught us to pray, "Thy kingdom come, Thy will be done in earth, as it is in heaven" (Matt. 6:10). We are compelling our opponent to fulfill the will of God, not our will. This is the reason for the war over mankind between God and Satan.

Jesus said:

Truly I tell you, among those born of women there has not risen anyone greater than John the Baptist; yet he who is least in the kingdom of heaven is greater than he. And from the days of John the Baptist until the present time, the kingdom of heaven has endured violent assault, and violent men seize it by force [as a precious prize—a share in the heavenly kingdom is sought with Most ardent zeal and intense exertion].

—MATTHEW 11:11–12, AMP

When referring to the kingdom of God in this book, I am talking about the divine authority and rule given by the Father to the Son. In Matthew 3:2, John the Baptist said, "Repent, for the kingdom of heaven is at hand" (NIV). Jesus proclaimed the kingdom saying, "The time is fulfilled" (Mark 1:15). The expression "the time is fulfilled" means the threshold of the powerful times we live in has suddenly been reached, the door is open, and the realization of the divine work of consummation is upon us.

What exactly did the people of Israel understand about this kingdom message?

- It was purely nationalistic.
- It would mean military, economic, and national restoration.
- It would be the restoration of God's righteous rule.

Jehovah's kingship was no problem; the difficulty arose in understanding the messianic reign of Jesus Christ. He came unto His own and they knew Him not.

> And as My Father has appointed a kingdom and conferred it on Me, so do I confer on you [the privilege and decree].
> —LUKE 22:29, AMP

Psalm 2 says this about the kingdom of God:

1. It will be similar to Israel: "Yet I have anointed (installed and placed) My king [firmly] on My holy hill of Zion" (Ps. 2:6, AMP).

2. It will involve world dominion: "Ask of Me, and I will give You the nations as Your inheritance, and the uttermost parts of the earth as Your possession" (Ps. 2:8, AMP).

3. It will be under the Messiah: "Why do the nations assemble with commotion [uproar and confusion of voices], and why do the people imagine (meditate upon and devise) an empty scheme? The kings of the earth take their places; the rulers take counsel together against the Lord and His Anointed One (the Messiah, the Christ). They say, Let us break Their bands [of restraint] asunder and cast Their cords [of control] from us. He Who sits in the heavens laughs; the Lord has them in derision [and in supreme contempt He mocks them]" (Ps. 2:1–4, AMP).

According to Revelation 11:15, the kingdom now controlled by men in opposition to God is to become the kingdom of our Lord and of His Christ. This Scripture goes on to say He shall reign forever and ever.

The kingdom of God brings "righteousness, peace and joy in the Holy Spirit" (Rom. 14:17, NIV). Entrance into the kingdom of God means deliverance from the power of darkness, according to Colossians 1:13, and is accomplished by the new birth mentioned in John 3:3, 5.[2]

Mature special ops Christians have sworn allegiance to Jesus Christ as Lord and King in the present war with Satan. They believe that the gospel is truly the good news about King Jesus and His kingdom. Their vision extends beyond the four walls of the church. They see the kingdom of God ruling and reigning over every aspect of life in every nation on the earth. They see a universal kingdom that extends to the far ends of every galaxy. This book is meant to encourage these special ops Christians with the revelation that they can have church in a way that promotes their gifts and the key objectives of Jesus Christ.

CHARACTERISTICS OF SPECIAL OPS CHRISTIANS:

1. Recognize kingdom authority but are often confused by church leadership

2. Run into confusing situations with church leaders who are worldly, manipulative, and binding

3. Are often anointed believers who find little in common with the contemporary programs and traditions of the local church

4. Are sometimes misunderstood and belong to the five-fold ministry of apostles, prophets, evangelists, pastors, or teachers, as recorded in Ephesians 4:12

5. Often pose a threat to church leaders who misunderstand them

6. Are sometimes ministers of the gospel who are advanced in their membership gifts, found in 1 Corinthians 12; their anointing often makes church leaders uncomfortable

7. Might be intercessors, prophetic personalities, and miracle workers

8. Their vision is often far-reaching and their sensitivity to the Spirit profound

9. Are the salt of the earth and are made of the same stuff that motivated the early church pioneers and original disciples of Jesus Christ

10. Value their growing relationship with their King more than life itself

11. Are usually driven by the words of Jesus Christ concerning the Great Commission to go and make disciples of men, as stated in Matthew 28:16–20 (AMP):

Now the eleven disciples went to Galilee, to the mountain to which Jesus had directed them and made appointment with them. And when they saw Him, they fell down and worshiped Him; but some doubted. Jesus approached and, breaking the silence, said to them, All authority (all power of rule) in heaven and on earth has been given to me. Go then and make disciples of all the nations, baptizing them into the name of the Father and of the Son and Holy Spirit, Teaching them to observe everything that I have commanded you, and behold, I am with you all the days (perpetually, uniformly, and on every occasion), to the [very] close and consummation of the age. Amen (so let it be).

CHAPTER 1

DEFINING *SPECIAL OPS*

Military Special Operations

"SPECIAL OPS" IS an abbreviation for the military term *special operations*. They are small, well-trained teams called upon to conduct difficult missions in enemy-controlled territory. Each branch of the military has a special ops group. The U.S. Navy has the SEALS, the Army has the Green Berets, and the Air Force has Pararescue units. My experience in special operations came as a Marine Corps Force Reconnaissance team leader in Vietnam. Force Reconnaissance was the most elite unit in the U. S. Marine Corps for many years. The Marine Corps has recently merged Force Reconnaissance into an expanded unit called Marine Corps Forces—Special Operations Command, or MARSOC. When functioning at full capacity, 2,500 highly trained marines, sailors, and civilian staff man MARSOC. Since the war on terror began, special operations units have increased in size in every branch of the military. These elite bands of warriors perform at high levels of proficiency. When the Marine Corps selects men and women for special ops service, they look for people comfortable with submitting to other skilled leaders. A lone ranger attitude and a lack of team spirit will get special ops candidates in all branches of service quickly dropped from the training unit.

There are three military concepts found in the Bible. Exodus 15:3 says, "The Lord is a Man of War" (AMP), and prominent biblical figures such as David, Deborah, Barak, Sampson, and Gideon were in the military.

The words *soldier, warfare,* and *war* occur many times in both the Old and New Testaments.

> **Soldier:** The word *soldier* in the Greek is *sartiotes*. It is used three times in the Book of Matthew, once in Mark, twice in Luke, and six times in John. The same word is used thirteen times in the book of Acts. *Soldier* is used metaphorically to represent one who endures hardship for the cause of Christ. In 2 Timothy 2:3 Paul says, "Take [with me] your share of hardships and suffering [which you are called to endure] as a good (first-class) soldier of Christ Jesus" (AMP).[1]

> **Warfare:** The Greek word for *warfare* is *strateia*, and it means "spiritual conflict." In 2 Corinthians 10:4 Paul says, "For the weapons of our warfare are not physical [weapons of flesh and blood], but they are mighty before God for the overthrow and destruction of strongholds" (AMP). In 1 Timothy 1:18 Paul continues the military theme by admonishing Timothy, "This charge and admonition I commit in trust to you, Timothy, my son, in accordance with the prophetic intimations which I formerly received concerning you, so that inspired and aided by them you may wage the good warfare" (AMP).[2]

> **War:** The Greek verb form of *war* is *strateuo*. It means to make war or to war metaphorically. The example for this kind of spiritual conflict can be found in 2 Corinthians 10:3, where Paul says, "For though we walk (live) in the flesh, we are not carrying on our war according to the flesh and using mere human weapons."[3]

Jesus Christ operated His earthly ministry like a special ops unit. He trained twelve disciples to operate in small groups, and they became extremely effective in carrying out His assignment. He used their gifts and developed them into a team that would take His message, the gospel, to the ends of the earth. Jesus truly used a special ops approach to spread His message to Israel and throughout the Roman Empire. He was in enemy-controlled territory for the entire three years of His ministry. But the special ops warrior runs most of his missions in territory controlled by the enemy. Jesus knew the spirit or potential evil that was in the men. He knew He was in the enemy's camp and conducted Himself accordingly.

Special ops Christians, first and foremost, are disciples who need a special ops church that will train them, but a disciple not only learns but also practices the teachings of Jesus Christ. Among many other things, he must be taught to operate in all the gifts of the Holy Spirit, as described in 1 Corinthians 12. How and by whom the special ops church teaches disciples to observe all that Jesus commanded can be found in Ephesians 4:11–16 (NIV).

> It was He [Jesus Christ] who gave some to be apostles, some to be prophets, some to be evangelists, and some to be pastors and teachers, to prepare God's people for works of service, so that the body of Christ may be built up until we all reach unity in the faith and in the knowledge of the Son of God and become mature, attaining to the whole measure of the fullness of Christ. Then we will no longer be infants, tossed back and forth by the waves, and blown here and there by every wind of teaching and by the cunning and craftiness of men in their deceitful scheming. Instead, speaking the truth in love, we will in all things grow up into him who is the Head, that is, Christ. From him the whole body, joined and held together by every supporting ligament, grows and builds itself up in love, as each part does its work.

The special ops church recognizes that the preparation of God's people for the work of service is a team effort according to Ephesians 4:11. Disciples are "to grow up into him who is the Head, that is Christ," under men and women who hold certain five-fold ministry offices. It is very clear that if the church has not attained to the whole measure of the fullness of Christ, the work of five-fold ministry is still necessary. The special ops church must realize: (1) "the unity in the faith," (2) "in the knowledge of the Son of God," (3) "become mature," (4) "attaining to the whole measure of the fullness of Christ" (Eph. 4:13, NIV). I know of no church, special ops or conventional, that has attained to the fullness of Christ. The church will make great strides toward fullness when it disciples the majority of its members.

Special ops churches are needed in every size. Both small and mega-size ministries can be special ops churches if the leadership is willing to train people to be disciples of Jesus. In small churches, nearly the entire congregation can be trained. Megachurches can train congregants for special operations because they usually have a vast pool of people—potential special ops Christians—from which to draw.

Special ops Christians are gifted to go places other Christians are not called to. For example, some special ops Christians are called to work in support roles. People in these positions should not be taken for granted, because they are vital to special operators working on the front lines carrying out the mission on local and international fronts. I have seen disciples in their eighties fulfilling their calling in support roles. Military logistics and supply also play major roles in every battle. There are many jobs available in the Lord's plan for His kingdom.

A special ops church is operational. Being operational means the church not only has a kingdom vision but a strong plan of action to carry it out. This book is designed to help churches identify and develop their special ops capability.

According the U.S. military, special ops units have fewer casualties, even though their mission is usually more dangerous. As you read this book, it will become apparent why their strategies and tactics are successful. Instructors for Marine Corps special ops training units employ an interesting method of weeding out troops not considered team players: they conduct exercises in long-distance swimming or a long run. The troop that comes in first and doesn't look over their shoulders to help other members is immediately dropped from the special ops training. The rest of the trainees get the message that the unit must work as a team.

I want to be very clear that rebellious people who claim to have a special portal to God and refuse to submit their gifts to a local church are not candidates to become special ops Christians. They are not disciples, and being a disciple is a prerequisite to success in special operations. Usually these types of people jump around from church to church, ministry to ministry, and create havoc with their super-spirituality. I refuse to endorse these people because they are usually not influenced by the Holy Spirit and because the fruit in their lives is non-existent.

A true special ops Christian looks for opportunities to be a team player in the local church. If a church fails to recognize the need for capable special ops Christians, it runs the risk of frustrating its disciples and eventually causing them to leave. Sometimes a local church will find itself in a "use them or lose them" situation. Marine Corps leaders are taught to keep their troops busy. When troops are not busy preparing for or running a mission, there is potential for them to become restless and negative. Remember the mission of the special ops Christian has everything to do with discipling the nations. A special ops church keeps its disciples operational by fulfilling a kingdom vision.

CHAPTER 2

SPECIAL OPS CHURCH

T HE SPECIAL OPS church is a church, as defined by the Greek word *ekklesia.* Special ops are the strategies and tactics adopted by a church in its pursuit to fulfill the great commission of Jesus Christ to disciple the nations.

Ekklesia makes reference to the whole company of the redeemed throughout the present era, the company to which Christ referred when He said in Matthew 16:18–19, "I will build my church and the gates of Hades (the powers of the infernal region) shall not overpower it [or be strong to its detriment or hold out against it]. I will give you the keys of the kingdom of heaven; and whatever you bind (declare to be improper and unlawful) on earth must be what is already bound in heaven: and whatever you loose (declare lawful) on earth must be what is already loosed in heaven" (AMP). A special ops church has the spiritual authority of the church to bind and loose. It is not a parachurch or just a ministry, and to become something less than a church could mean forfeiting its authority and protection.[1]

And He has put all things under His feet and has appointed Him the universal and supreme Head of the church [a headship exercised throughout the church].

—EPHESIANS 1:22, AMP

In the singular, *ekklesia* represents a company consisting of professed believers. In the New Testament, *ekklesia* is used to refer to the congregation the living God assembles about His Messiah, Jesus. The church is the spiritual family of God, with Christian fellowship created by the Holy Spirit in Christ Jesus. The mystery of the church exists wherever the Holy Spirit unites worshiping Christians together.[2]

Take care and be on guard for yourselves and the whole flock over which the Holy Spirit has appointed you bishops and guardians, to shepherd (tend and feed and guide) the church of the Lord or of God which He obtained for Himself [buying it and saving it for Himself] with His own blood.

—Acts 20:28, amp

To the church (assembly) of God which is in Corinth, to those consecrated and purified and made holy in Christ Jesus, [who are] selected and called to be saints (God's people), together with all those who in any place call upon and give honor to the name of our Lord Jesus Christ, both their Lord and ours.

—1 Corinthians 1:2, amp

The special ops church can be greatly assisted in fulfilling its role in the Great Commission by pursuing the objectives of the kingdom of God within the framework of the following scriptures, strategies, and tactics.

1. The church is built upon the foundation of the apostles and prophets, with Jesus Christ Himself as the chief Cornerstone (Eph. 2:20).

2. The church must follow a clear mission and vision in its effort to disciple the nations (Matt. 28:18–20).

3. The church should be obedient to the following guiding
   principles:
   - code of conduct: accountability, loyalty, integrity,
     and teamwork
   - rules of conduct: the nine principles of war (unity of
     command, objective, offensive, mass-power, economy
     of force, maneuver, security, surprise, simplicity)[3]

UNITED STATES MARINE CORPS SPECIAL OPS

Much of what I share in this book comes out of my own personal
experiences as a former U.S. Marine Corps combat officer and after
forty years of ministry in the church. I served in special ops as a
Marine Corps Force Recon team leader in 1969 during the Vietnam
War. I led twenty-three missions of six and eight-man teams deep
into enemy territory. I learned how to successfully plan and execute
missions with a small team of disciplined and dedicated marines. The
foundation of the United States Marine Corps is built on a six-man
squad. Four such squads make up a platoon. No matter how large the
unit gets, the squad, known as a fire team, is still the backbone of the
Marine Corps. The U.S. Marine Corps has probably been one of the
most successful military organizations in history. It uses a combat
doctrine of honor, courage, and commitment to make disciples of
men and women in the corps.

Experience has taught me that successful special ops missions can
change the outcome of a war in profound ways. My 161-man unit, First
Force Recon Company, was awarded a meritorious unit citation for
combat action in the central highlands of Vietnam in 1969. Out of 161
men, about sixty were operational in the field while about one hundred
worked in support positions. The following recommendation, dated
March 10, 1970, serves as an example of how a small, highly disciplined, and committed organization of marine disciples can produce
tremendous results in battle. Small special ops churches or megachurches with a recognized and highly trained special ops capability
can have the same results in their mission to disciple the nations. Try

to draw the analogy between natural and spiritual warfare from this citation.

FIRST FORCE RECON COMPANY'S MERITORIOUS UNIT COMMENDATION RECOMMENDATION

The specific missions of First Force Recon Company ranged from penetration of deep and long-range reconnaissance patrols into the very heart of enemy-controlled territory to locate enemy troop concentrations and to the capture of enemy personnel. In the face of numerically superior enemy forces who were employing aggressive, well-trained counter-reconnaissance forces, the company repeatedly reentered enemy sanctuaries, completing assigned missions and providing information vital to the subsequent fixing, interdiction and destruction of untold numbers of enemy forces. Accomplishing a total of 191 patrols, the information gathered by these patrols formed the foundation and impetus for operations and massive air/artillery strikes against enemy base camps, lines of communications and supply depots. The identity and location of the newly infiltrated 90th NVA regiment into Quang Nam Province, the egress of the 21st and 1st NVA Regiments from Quang Nam Province and subsequent return of these units was established in large measure by information gathered by the company's patrols. Intelligence gathered from information provided by these patrols went on to precipitate highly successful forays, including Operation Durham Peak, by the 1st Marine Division into the Que Son Mountains and Antenna Valley area where extremely complex enemy base camps and large quantities of supplies were uncovered and destroyed. The enemy was denied a vital stepping-stone to Da Nang from the south and to An Hoa from the east and his designs for offensive operations against these areas were effectively pre-empted. While embarked on operations for the 3rd Marine Amphibious Force, the company was to locate the enemy's Military Region 5 and Front Four Headquarters, their related installations and supply and communications routes in the south-western reaches of Quang Nam Province. Patrols provided a flow of heretofore unknown and extremely valuable information from the interior of the enemy's base areas. With repeated interdiction of his newly identified installations, and facilities, the enemy was effectively kept off balance and rendered unable to launch a "1969 summer offensive" of the magnitude he had intended.[4]

The following seven points break down the approach of the First Force Special Ops and why it was awarded a Meritorious Unit Commendation.

- First Force ran deep reconnaissance patrols into the heart of enemy-controlled areas.
- In spite of enemy efforts to keep First Force out, the special ops marines continued to penetrate the enemy's sanctuaries with accurate air and artillery assaults.
- Information from the patrols was the impetus for further offensive operations.
- The First Marine Division used First Force's information to go after the enemy with thousands of conventional marines that helped friendly villagers establish themselves in the region and then begin to occupy.
- The identity of enemy units was uncovered by First Force's deep reconnaissance.
- Information was gathered from the interior of the enemy's strongholds.
- The enemy was unable to go on the offensive in the summer of 1969, and First Force was credited with

SPECIAL OPS CHURCH

keeping the enemy off balance with its special ops
approach to war.

In light of the information in this citation, a special ops Christian
should be able to recognize the spiritual significance of how a special
ops church can also be highly effective in a battle against the powers
of darkness. The special ops church can open up enemy-controlled
areas so the church can grow and take dominion. A special ops church
with less than two hundred people or a megachurch with thousands
of congregants can accomplish amazing feats in establishing God's
kingdom in the earth by adopting certain warfare-related tactics and
strategies.

In recent years, I have been able to incorporate the special ops
concept I learned in Vietnam into my ministry. In twenty-four
months of using the strategy, we have built ten church/daycare build-
ings in South Africa while planting half dozen churches in Southern
California. Using South Africa as a launch area, we have moved into
Zambia, Mozambique, southern Uganda, and northern Rwanda. We
wanted to use the love of Jesus Christ to win the hearts and minds of
people and nations at risk. In this book, I plan to share concepts and
principles that can help create a special ops-capable church.

There is a paradigm shift occurring in the church. It is part of His
overall plan to fulfill the Great Commission. Special ops churches or
church departments must be able to change from the old, inflexible
church paradigm to a new, more flexible model that produces disciplined, highly trained people. There is no room in a special ops church
for a lot of unnecessary drama. Normal growing pains that mature
the saints in the work of the ministry is to be expected, but chronic
Jezebel and disruptive spirits are not welcome. Remember, special ops
capability is built on Jesus Christ, the chief Cornerstone of the church,
by His loyal disciples.

We live in a very dangerous world. In every war, military leadership must work with political leaders to establish a grand strategic
objective. If there are too many unnecessary distractions to leaders
and followers in the local church, their focus can be shattered and

18

missions abandoned. My definition of church drama is when immaturity overwhelms the mission of the church and prohibits it from carrying out the Great Commission. A megachurch must shelter its special ops capability from much of the normal church drama. It should identify its special ops church capability through the department it develops for their five-fold ministers and special ops church members who serve in that department. A special ops department can be advertised and church members could apply. A screening board led by seasoned apostles and prophets could act in the selection process of those church members who fit the special ops church mission. A pure special ops church must maintain order, sometimes at the expense of church growth. When programs or secondary missions of a church do not relate to the fulfillment of the grand strategic objective of Jesus Christ, inventory must be taken and adjustments made to the agenda of that church.

The Great Commission is the grand strategic objective of Jesus Christ, and the church must be held accountable to carry it out. The Great Commission dictates the purpose for which every other mission, goal, or objective of the church exists. Keeping this in view will enable the special ops church to be very effective in its effort to follow the Lord Jesus Christ in His plan to see nations discipled.

> Go then and make disciples of all the nations, baptizing them into the name of the Father and Son and Holy Spirit, Teaching them to observe everything that I have commanded you, and behold, I am with you all the days (perpetually, uniformly, and on every occasion), to the [very] close and consummation of the age.
>
> —MATTHEW 28:19–20, AMP

RESPECT FOR THE LORD OF HOSTS

Respect and honor of rank is something desperately needed in the church today. Although we are equal in redemption as brothers and sisters in Christ, we must recognize the rank an officer in the body of Christ wears. We salute the office, not the man.

The Lord Jesus Christ, also known as the Prince of the Lord's host, is the commander and great strategist for His church. We would do well to remember Joshua's encounter with the Lord, the warrior Prince.

> When Joshua was by Jericho, he looked up, and behold, a Man stood near him with His drawn sword in His hand. And Joshua went to Him and said to Him, Are you for us or for our adversaries? And He said, No [neither], but as Prince of the Lord's host have I now come. And Joshua fell on his face to the earth and worshiped, and said to Him, What says my Lord to His servant? And the Prince of the Lord's host said to Joshua, Loose your shoes from off your feet, for the place where you stand is holy. And Joshua did so.
>
> —JOSHUA 5:13–15, AMP

Joshua was a seasoned special ops man. Remember his reconnaissance mission into the Promised Land with Caleb and the ten unbelievers. (See Numbers 14:6–9.) Joshua was a true disciple by the time he reached Jericho. He knew about respect, tactics, strategy, and obedience. He knew how to subordinate himself immediately to the Prince of the Lord's host. He was totally focused, and after forty years of living in the wilderness, all church drama had pretty much ceased.

Holy ground is where special ops Christians and the special ops church find themselves when receiving war plans from the Prince of the Lord's host. The Man with the sword in His hand was not a mere angel, because He accepted Joshua's homage of worship. Joshua encountered Jesus Christ in His warrior mode. It is time for the church to loosen her shoes and take them off, because where she stands is holy. It is a place of humility where she must change Her battle plan for a more current plan prepared especially by Christ, the Prince of the Lord's host.

Although special ops Christianity is a team effort, there is a chain of command. With every military mission, there must be a clear authority structure. As a lieutenant in Vietnam I was the team leader in the field. I received my orders from my commanding officer, a major, and he received them from the commanding general of the First Marine Division. Jesus Christ is our commanding general, and apostles and prophets of various rank and experience are stationed in the chain of command as the Holy Spirit directs. They receive battle plans from the Prince of the Lord's host.

> Therefore you are no longer outsiders (exiles, migrants, and aliens, excluded from the rights of citizens), but you now share citizenship with the saints (God's own people, consecrated and set apart for Himself); and you belong to God's [own] household. You are built upon the foundation of the apostles and prophets with Christ Jesus Himself the chief Cornerstone. In him the whole structure is joined (bound, welded) together harmoniously, and it continues to rise (grow, increase) into a holy temple in the Lord [a sanctuary dedicated, consecrated, and sacred to the presence of the Lord]. In Him [and in fellowship with one another] you yourselves also are being built up [into this structure] with the rest, to form a fixed abode (dwelling place) of God in (by, through) the Spirit.
>
> —EPHESIANS 2:19–22, AMP

In this season of church history, true apostles and prophets are those who have been mentored and taught over the years by members of the five-fold ministry. These men and women have had spiritual parents, aunts, and uncles disciple them in leadership for such a time as this. Their character and relationship with the Lord Jesus are their primary credentials and qualify them to lead His army into battle. The size of their ministry or church has nothing to do with their credibility or what makes them capable of leading a battle. Modern-day apostles and prophets must have a pure heart as disciples of the Lord Jesus Christ. Although apostles and prophets should be team players, they also are master builders. The team must rely upon them for overall direction, strategy, and tactics in the battle.

> So God has appointed some in the church [for His own use]: first apostles (special messengers); second prophets (inspired preachers and expounders); third teachers; then wonder-workers; then those with ability to heal the sick; helpers; administrators; [speakers in] different (unknown) tongues. Are all apostles (special messengers)? Are all prophets (inspired interpreters of the will and purposes of God): Are all teachers? Do all have the power of performing miracles? Do all possess extraordinary powers of healing? Do all speak with tongues? Do all interpret? But earnestly desire and zealously cultivate the greatest and best gifts and graces (the higher gifts and the choicest graces). And yet I will show you a still more excellent way [one that is better by far and highest of them all—love].
>
> —1 CORINTHIANS 12:28–32, AMP

Truly the army of God is a team sport. God chooses the gifts we will operate in. It is our responsibility to desire the greater gifts. The greater gift is always the one needed at the moment. The point man on patrol with me in Vietnam had to operate at a high level of training because he would be the first team member to confront the enemy in a firefight. The radioman was of equal importance to me because he was responsible for communicating with our command and communications bunker, located twenty to fifty miles away. I was anointed and commissioned to design and lead the patrol by making key decisions along the way. The army of God must operate in a similar fashion. Although we are all equal in redemption, we are called and appointed by God to function at different levels of authority in His kingdom.

We were taught in the Marine Corps Officer Candidates School (OCS) at Quantico, Virginia, that a leader rarely asked one of his subordinates to do something he wouldn't do himself. We were taught right from the beginning to make sure our troops had eaten before we put a fork to our mouths. It started at OCS, where our drill instructor, or DI, checked the quality of food we were about to be served at the mess hall. Then the DI would carefully watch as we passed through the chow line. Once the platoon was seated and eating, the DI would move through the chow line and fill his tray with the same food we were eating. I have always found it hard in the church world to be honored by people directing me to the head of the buffet line. I am always very uncomfortable with this kind of honor because marines are taught to be servant leaders. We were taught to suffer with our men in combat. The seat of honor for a marine is one that is right in the middle of the battle with his men.

> By faith Moses, when he was come to years, refused to be called the son of Pharaoh's daughter; Choosing rather to suffer affliction with the people of God, than to enjoy the pleasures of sin for a season; Esteeming the reproach of Christ greater riches than the treasurers in Egypt: for he had respect unto the recompense of the reward.
>
> —HEBREWS 11:24–26

Moses truly had the stuff great military generals are made of. He chose to suffer affliction with God's people. Apostolic leadership in the special ops church is no cakewalk.

At sixty years old, I found myself racing to get out of Mozambique before dark because the police had threatened to arrest my team and I. My wife, Barbara, and I skirted the Hillbrough area of Johannesburg ten nights in a row. That area is one of the most dangerous in the world. We have taken flights to Africa while our U.S. military forces were landing in Afghanistan and Iraq. These missions would have been a lot easier twenty years ago, but our call was for this millennium and a time such as this. It is one thing to wear the rank of a senior officer in the body of Christ and another thing to do it with honor by leading like Moses.

Warrior Leaders Birth Warrior Leaders

I've been in ministry for more than forty years, and I have seen several movements in the body of Christ that attempted to birth the army of God. In recent years, there has been a lot of talk about warriors in the church. There has been a lot of posturing and saber rattling, but I must admit most of it has been a pathetic, wannabe or pretender mentality that turns a lot of good people off. I learned through Marine Corps special ops in the Vietnam War that either you were a committed warrior or you were not a real warrior at all.

Warriors Are Loved or Hated but Never Ignored

The Merriam-Webster Dictionary defines a warrior as a man engaged or experienced in warfare.[5] *Engaged* is probably the operative word in this definition. Experience in warfare comes from engaging in warfare. When church leaders are unwilling or unable to engage in spiritual warfare, the people following them will not be able to become warriors because there is no spiritual impartation. Committed warrior leaders give birth to committed warrior leaders. Tribulation and controversy are part of the nature of the call to be a true warrior.

> Wherein ye greatly rejoice, though now for a season, if need be, ye are in heaviness through manifold temptation. That the trial of your faith, being much more precious than of gold that perisheth, though it be tried with fire, might be found unto praise and honour and glory at the appearing of Jesus Christ.
>
> —1 Peter 1:6–7

It is not impossible to train people on the job in the midst of a battle. I remember in June 1969 I had to walk not only as the team leader but also the point man while training a young marine. Point man is not a good role for a reconnaissance team leader because he could be killed or wounded in a point contact with the enemy. Then the team will greatly miss his leadership in accomplishing the mission deep in enemy-controlled territory. Necessity or field expediency sometimes forces us to handle certain action above and beyond the call of duty, and this was one of those times. We must train our special ops Christians to respond to the battles we will face in pursuit of the Great Commission. Often the church looks more like a college fraternity party than the disciplined army of God. Hopefully the following chapters will reveal some of the foundational information necessary for a mighty army of Special Ops Christians to come forth in the body of Christ.

THE ART AND SCIENCE OF WAR

The art of war and the science of war are driven by the mission, vision, and guiding principles of the special ops church. Besides the mission and vision (which will be discussed in the next chapter), the art and science of war are also subject to the guiding principles of the special ops church, known as the code of conduct and the rules of conduct.

The art of war can often be most easily recognized in the development of foot soldiers and their advancement in battle. The science of war in natural warfare deals more with high-tech weapons and sophisticated intelligence-gathering methods. These are the product of gifted minds that work at very high levels of insight and creativity.

In the special ops church, the art of war can be observed in the activity of the foot soldiers, such as the apostles, teachers, and pastors that execute most of the church planting and management among the nations. The science of war in the special ops church can often be identified in the work of the prophets, evangelists, intercessors, and miracle workers that operate at very high levels of the seer gifts, and signs and wonders. Their activity can be likened to the smart bombs, stealth aircraft, and missiles used in natural warfare. The art of war and science of war work together and are not exclusive of each other.

The five-fold minister can operate in one or all of the ministry offices of apostle, prophet, evangelist, pastor, and teacher. This means that a five-fold minister can at times work in both the art and science of war as they move through a specific mission. Member gifts, as found in 1 Corinthians 12:1–31, can also be employed in the art and science of war by any special ops Christian in accordance with the authority of the believer.

We see the art of war more as the foot soldier moves forward on the ground, while the science of war deals more with air superiority. We know that spiritual warfare definitely takes place on the earth as well as in the heavenlies. Often the air battle deals with the displacement of powers and principalities in the heavenlies (Eph. 6:12), while ground troops using the art of war are busy moving forward, taking territories with the gospel of Jesus Christ. Air superiority aids the foot soldier with the battles that are fought spiritually in the heavens and with those battles that are fought on Earth. Spiritual warfare, like natural warfare, should be fought using the principle that he who controls the battle in the heavens usually wins the battle on the earth. Worship, prayer, and declarations using the Word of God are spiritual weapons that give the special ops Christian air superiority.

COALITION WARFARE

Coalition: a union or a temporary union for a common purpose[6]

> On April 23, 1969, my six-man recon team, Hanover Sue, was sent into enemy-controlled territory along a dry riverbed about twenty miles south west of Da Nang, South Vietnam. Soon after disembarking from a CH-46 helicopter, a squad of enemy North Vietnamese army regulars began to follow my team. I radioed for help from the gun bird helicopters flying cover for the CH-46s. The gun birds responded by firing rockets about forty meters behind the team so we could break contact with the enemy squad and continue our mission. The rockets started a fire. The wind began to blow the flames in our direction, causing the dry grass and brush to catch fire. The enemy then summoned more soldiers and began to fan the flames in our direction with the help of the

wind. As the wall of flame approached my team, I ordered our point to lead us up a rocky hill that could give us our best chance of escape. The flames followed us up the hill like they had a life of their own. We ducked into a shallow ravine using the rocks for cover and concealment. The enemy and the fire swept by us. We moved out of the ravine and followed the enemy to the top of the hill where they broke off in different directions looking for us. Now we owned the top of the hill, where we would stay until dark. At dusk the flames of the fire began to move back up the hill with another group of enemy soldiers fanning the blaze.

We knew at that point the enemy was going to continue to hunt for us the entire night. I called for air support. Just as the enemy was moving within twenty meters of the team's position, I heard the voice of an Air Force Spooky pilot come over my radio. He said, "Where are you, Hanover Sue? I understand you got a little unwelcome company down there." Spooky was a heavily armed, fixed-wings gunship that had just rained down machine gun power. I turned on my strop light, which could only be seen from the air.

The pilot said, "I have your position. Now tell me, how far outside your perimeter are they?"

I said, "Twenty meters."

He said, "Get the team down and don't anyone move." With those words, Spooky rained down fire twenty meters outside our perimeter. The enemy would not move and used the rocks for cover. For the next eight hours, through occasional heavy cloud cover, Spooky continued his assault on the enemy around us.

When dawn arrived, the slow-flying Spooky had to leave us for fear of being shot out of the sky by enemy anti-aircraft gunners that had set up in the area. Just as Air Force Spooky was leaving, the pilot reassured me help was on the way in the form of the Fifth Marine Regiment that was moving toward our position at first light. We could see MedEvac helicopters landing and taking off in the distance from our position on the high hill. The Fifth Marine's infantry unit was now running through the jungle to assist my beleaguered team. This was coalition warfare in high gear. First the air force had saved us from the enemy's night assault and fire. Now the marine infantry was losing men to heatstroke as they desperately moved toward our hilltop.

The enemy saw what had come to our aid and made one more assault on our position. Enemy AK-47 round skipped off the rocks all around my point man and I as we ran across the hilltop. The enemy was now inside our perimeter taking up positions in the rocks. A blast of enemy machine gun fire knocked my point man off his feet. I instinctively pulled the pin on a grenade and tossed it into the rocks in front of us. Trying to tend to my wounded point man, shout orders to the team, and ask for more air support over the radio was no small task. Finally a different voice came over the radio identifying himself as the company commander with the Fifth Marine Regiment. He said, "We are coming up the hill. Don't shoot us." Within minutes, like ants, there were U.S. marines without helmets or flack jackets all over that hill. They had tossed their equipment so that they could make the run up the hill in time to save my team, and they did.[7]

It is this kind of coalition warfare the church needs to get a hold of. If the church ran its operations and fought the way the air force and marines do, there would be great success. The church is usually found competing with itself when it should be involved in building Christian operational coalitions. The Father, Son, and Holy Spirit are a perfect example of a successful coalition. Remember the Merriam-Webster Dictionary says *coalition* means "union," which is "the act or instance of uniting two or more things into one."[8]

When we look at the grand strategic objective the Lord has given the church, we begin to understand why Jesus prayed the following prayer in John 17:18-22:

> Just as you sent Me into the world, I also have sent them into the world. And so for their sake and on their behalf I sanctify (dedicate, consecrate) Myself, that they also may be sanctified (dedicated, consecrated, made holy) in the Truth. Neither for these alone do I pray [it is not for their sake only that I make this request], but also for all those who will ever come to believe in (trust in, cling to, rely on) me through their word and teaching, That they all may be one, [just] as You, Father, are in Me and I in you, that they also may be one in Us, so that the world may believe and be convinced that You have sent Me. I have given to them the glory and honor which You have given Me, that they may be One [even] as We are one: I in them and You in Me, in order that they may become one and perfectly united, that the world may know and [definitely] recognize that You sent Me and that You have loved them [even] as you have loved Me.

Jesus was well aware of the importance of training His special ops team to be unified. Jesus knew His disciples would have to be one even as He and His Father were one if they were going to be successful in completing the church's objective. It is going to take coalitions of Christians to bring about victory in the battle to win the hearts and minds of the people of the nations with the love of Jesus Christ. This is not a time for churches to think they can pull off the objective single-handedly. Christians must find common ground in the battle and be willing to form meaningful coalitions for common purposes. Unity in the body of Christ is possible because Jesus has already asked the Father for great unity among His disciples.

Having a special ops mentality has allowed our Angel Fire Coalition of Churches—a group I have the honor of leading—to accomplish great things not only in the U.S. but also in Mexico, Peru, and on the continent of Africa. From our Angel Fire mother church in Simi

Valley, California, about three miles north of the Ronald Reagan Presidential Library, we have planted six other special ops churches that have joined us in our effort to help accomplish the Great Commission. We are currently committed to building hundreds of multi-service church/daycare structures around the world. During our first twenty-four months of service in South Africa, ten structures were built, totaling ten thousand square feet of construction. The structures were built in some of the poorest black townships near Johannesburg. Many of our African hosts have told us what we were able to accomplish in such a short amount of time was unprecedented in that region of the world.

I happened to be in Washington D.C. during the Desert Storm battle in Kuwait and Iraq. I was invited to dinner by one of General Colin Powell's staff officers during one of the most intense times of that war. General Powell was commanding a coalition of allied forces that quickly ended Saddam Hussein's occupation in Kuwait and nearly destroyed Iraq's army in just a few days. During the dinner, my interest was piqued concerning coalition warfare as my host, a senior staff officer from Powell's strategy committee, described the general's outstanding leadership. The more he spoke about the power of coalition warfare, the more my spirit witnessed to what he was saying. I began to see the church's need to wake up and move into spiritual warfare and kingdom missions as a coalition. I began to envision projects impossible for churches and ministries to complete suddenly finished by coalitions formed by God's people. I began to see the kingdom of God registering great victories all over the world.

Coalition warfare is just a larger example of how five-fold ministry is supposed to operate. When apostles, prophets, evangelists, pastors, and teachers work as a team, great things are accomplished in the church. The same is true about church and ministry coalitions. Members of a coalition can often bring much more to the table in terms of supply and gifting than any single church. Coalitions can knock down denominational barriers concerning kingdom-based issues. Coalitions dealing with humanitarian causes such as AIDS orphans in Africa can drop the sectarian rhetoric and deliver the supplies needed to save the children. Coalitions of independent churches and ministries offer even greater potential for success in faith-based humanitarian efforts worldwide.

Jesus prayed in John 17 for the unity of His disciples. Has there ever been a greater need in the church for unity and coalition warfare against the kingdom of darkness than now?

More and more over the years, my wife Barbara and I have needed to use a private airplane to get to South Africa. In August 2006 we desperately needed to get to Johannesburg to attend a key meeting that would launch our Children's Village in Soweto. The Children's Village was to be home to about 150 orphans. It was also designed as a model of how to run a sustainable facility that would shelter, feed, and clothe orphans and also provide them with educational and medical aid. We were working against time to have the village operational by 2010 for the World Cup soccer matches in South Africa. We wanted people from different nations attending the games to see something could be done to ease the suffering of the 12 million AIDS orphans in sub-Saharan Africa. This was a very important mission. Barbara had been severely injured in a head-on automobile accident and had a valid need for a private jet to avoid further injury to her legs. We flew economy part of the way, and Barbara suffered a lot of pain on the twenty-two-hour flight to Johannesburg and the twenty-two-hour flight back to Los Angeles. Nonetheless, like a true special ops woman, she completed the two-week mission.

AIR SUPPORT IS SOMETIMES VITAL FOR A SPECIAL OPS MISSION

My need to protect Barbara from further injury got me thinking about coalition warfare and war in general. When I was on a mission deep in enemy-controlled territory in Vietnam and I needed air support, I got it from the marines, navy, or air force. When I needed help in combat, the different services would send phantom jets and helicopters. They sent help because of the contribution I was making in fighting the war. They didn't ignore me or treat me like a faithless

31

beggar because I didn't own an airplane. I believe what Barbara and I and other special ops Christians are doing to save orphans in Africa is extremely important. It is more important than what I did in Vietnam and in some ways just as dangerous. Wouldn't it be strategic if those owning airplanes in the body of Christ began to recognize the mission of its special ops Christians and offered their planes to be used in key special ops missions? Often, airplanes belonging to wealthy ministries are used to fly preachers around the world to hold evangelistic crusades. Airplanes are part of the science of war. They are ultimately purchased with God's money. Those stewarding them need to reach out to God's special ops church and lend their support, providing air support where it is most needed.

Owning a multi-million dollar airplane is a huge responsibility. Duty dictates that these strategic assets should cover elite special ops Christians risking their lives in foreign lands. It is imperative that true, apostolic, wealthy leadership in the body of Christ recognize the value of special ops Christians. We are finding and closing in on the enemy in key battlefronts worldwide. Special ops Churches will need the recognition of larger expressions of the body of Christ to bring about major victories planned by Jesus for His kingdom. I believe one of the signs of true apostolic anointing in this church age is the ability of apostles to connect with the international spiritual battlefield and respond properly with supply.

CHAPTER 3

MISSION, VISION, AND GUIDING PRINCIPLES

*External religious worship [religion as it is expressed in
outward acts] that is pure and unblemished in the sight of
God the Father is this: to visit and help and care for the
orphans and widows in their affliction and need, and to keep
oneself unspotted and uncontaminated from the world.*

JAMES 1:27, AMP

THE CHILDREN'S MISSION, A GIFT FROM GOD

I WOULD LIKE TO share with the reader a history of the Children's Village project I mentioned in the previous chapter. In January 2005, just when my wife Barbara and I were comfortable building multi-service, church/daycare structures in South Africa, the Lord challenged us with a new mission. During a breakfast meeting in Johannesburg with Dr. Mark Ottenweiler of Hope Worldwide, we learned there were 1,200,000 orphans in South Africa. He went on to tell us there were over 12 million orphans in sub-Saharan Africa. Dr. Ottenweiler explained that the vast majority of these children had lost both parents to AIDS. After breakfast, Barbara and I returned to our hotel room. We sat quietly, and finally Barbara broke the silence saying, "Well, I think the Lord is asking for more of us than just daycare centers here."

That evening at a conference in the black township of Tskane, Apostle John Mubunda, a member of our Angel Fire Coalition—South

Africa ushered me into a back room for a meeting. Two women dressed in modest but colorful African attire had requested to speak with me privately. Their hearts were broken for the poor, especially the orphans in their community. The women never stopped weeping as they shared their burden. They wanted me to go back to the U.S. and share their burden with President George W. Bush. Immediately I discerned that it wasn't George Bush the Lord was commissioning to help the orphans. It was Barbara and I. This experience was very humbling.

The next day we were traveling around Soweto with another member of our coalition, Apostle John Mutula. I asked him to take me to see land he owned on the west side of the township. When I mentioned the great need of the orphans in South Africa, Apostle Mutula and his wife, Thandie, got very excited. Thandie had been carrying a great burden for the orphans and didn't know what to do for them. While Barbara and I walked the land with the Mutulas, I began to share my vision for the Children's Village being built on the property. Immediately the Mutuals dedicated the land for the eventual construction of the orphanage. There on that land Barbara and I made a covenant with the couple to do everything in our power to see the Children's Village built for 150 orphans. Before we returned to the U.S., we had two more pieces of property pledged for Children's Villages. Each village would cost about $300,000 to build, which was sixty times the cost of our first multi-service structure. One of these villages seemed impossible to build, let alone multiple villages. It was going to take everything Barbara and I had learned over the years to successfully pull off this mission.

Yes, we beat our deadline of having the village ready to show the world during the 2010 World Cup soccer matches, and today that Children's Village is standing proud on that land. During playtime the laughter of 150 children fills the neighborhood surrounding the village. Plans for the construction of three more villages have already been filed.

DIVINE APPOINTMENTS LAUNCH SPECIAL OPS CHURCHES INTO INTERNATIONAL MISSIONS

Let me share a little more history on how we got involved in South Africa. The vision for South Africa began early in 2000 at the home of our spiritual parents, Rey and Lois Soto, in Palos Verdes Estates, California. For years we had gathered every Wednesday evening at the Soto's home for a lavish dinner, prayer, and Bible study. One evening at the gathering, Pete Samra, a man Barbara and I had ordained into the ministry, had just returned from South Africa. He was about ready to give the group a report on his missionary work when he pulled me aside and whispered in my ear. He said, "Bill, did you know we can build church and daycare structures for about five thousand dollars each in South Africa?" This was true because the exchange rate was fifteen Rand to one dollar at the time. In recent years it has averaged about seven Rand to one dollar. After a short report Pete turned the meeting over to me with Rey and Lois' permission. I couldn't help myself. I went into a prophetic mode, telling the twenty-five people gathered there that we needed to build one hundred church/daycare centers in South Africa. That night, $2,500 was placed on a coffee table in the center of the Sotos's living room, and we were suddenly in the church building business using our non-profit corporation, Angel Fire Fellowship, as the vehicle to collect funding for the project. During the next five years, Barbara and I would have to walk through cancer and automobile accidents. A major disappointment was the many people who walked away from Angel Fire Christian Center, our headquarters in Simi Valley, California, because they couldn't handle the battle and our commitment to God's kingdom plan for it.

MISSION DEFINES THE REASON SPECIAL OPS CHURCH EXISTS

Mission, according to the Webster's Dictionary, among other definitions, is simply a task.[1] Warriors only engage in war when it advances the mission they have been given. When I served in special ops with the Marine Corps Elite First Force Recon Company, we had a clear mission for every deep-reconnaissance patrol we ran. We knew where we were going and what we were going to do when we got there. We knew how to engage the enemy and how to disengage depending upon the mission. We knew how to maneuver when our plan wasn't working. My platoon sergeant, Gene Ayers, and I would rehearse our team members until we felt that every man knew his role on the mission. Special ops can eliminate heavy friendly casualties with a clear mission and vision for what the team needs to do to accomplish the grand strategic objective. In like manner, a violation of mission, vision, and other key principles can mean disaster for special operators.

The success of a special ops church begins when every special ops Christian involved has a clear understanding of the mission. It takes disciples who are willing to be trained to engage the enemy anywhere in the world in pursuit of the mission. The special ops church needs the semper fidelas—"always faithful"—spirit of the United States Marine Corps.

The following accounts of my true-life experience in war will be used to highlight some very important principles concerning the successful accomplishment of the mission. Once again try to relate the example of natural warfare to what we encounter in spiritual warfare. Often the accomplishment of the mission in spiritual warfare is very practical in nature. Discipline and training can carry us quite a way in battle.

> From April 13 to April 17, 1969, an eight-man special ops Marine Corps Force Recon team laid facedown and undetected inside a North Vietnamese regimental base camp not far from the Laotian Border. During this five-day patrol deep in enemy-controlled territory, thousands of enemy troops moved within forty feet of the team's position over a five-day period of time. I was the assistant team leader during this daring mission. We were to engage the enemy by observing him, and observe is what we did. This special ops patrol existed for one primary mission, that was, to

observe the enemy. Although this was a totally covert mission, we were expected to protect ourselves against any enemy incursion into our position. The team survived the ordeal because every member understood the mission. There was no confusion as to whether the mission called for us to grab a prisoner, bomb, or engage in an all-out fire fight with our adversaries. Most of the daylight hours, an enemy trail monitor stood just forty feet from our position...located in a small tree line. It would not have been difficult to take him prisoner, but any misstep would have caused hundreds of enemy soldiers to converge on us and wipe out our team. We were twenty-five miles behind enemy lines with jungles, mountain ranges, and huge rivers between us and our First Force Recon Company headquarters at a place called An Hoa, South Vietnam. Our commanding officer reminded us several times during the five-day ordeal to stick to our mission and just observe the enemy. In the early morning hours of the fifth day, we moved to a bomb crater just two hundred meters from our position, where a CH-46 helicopter lifted us out of enemy camp trapeze-style with a 140-foot cable ladder. Phantom Marine Corps jet aircraft ran air strikes to distract the enemy. Remarkable? Yes. The key to our mission was discipline and obedience. The success of our mission allowed the First Marine Division Air Wing to use the science of war to extract us out of the lion's mouth. They skillfully positioned jet aircraft and helicopters between our team and the enemy as we were lifted above the jungle canopy. Then B-52 bombers that had left Thailand many hours before showed up at the right time to unload one thousand-pound bombs on the enemy base camp we had vacated just moments before.[2]

When a special ops church is clear about its mission, it can become successful in the execution of that mission. Remember the mission of a special ops church must always be in direct support of Christ's overall grand strategic objective, which is the Great Commission. For instance, the mission of Angel Fire Christian Center is to:

- develop people from every nation morally, mentally, and physically and to imbue them with an unconditional love for mankind found in the Father, Son, and the Holy Spirit.
- engender in people's character the highest responsibilities of command, citizenship, and government.
- share the presence, power, and glory of God in our mission to help disciple the nations.

The language of this mission statement certainly coincides with the Great Commission. Phrases such as *developing people* and *imbuing them with unconditional love for mankind,* and *engendering their character* are totally consistent with Christ's grand strategic objective. The mission statement of a special ops church must always flow upward and into the Great Commission.

This mission statement calls for more than holding large crusades and seeing thousands of souls saved. This statement calls us to disciple people and nations. It calls not just for converts to Christianity but disciples. It calls for apostolic action and anointing. We will develop this thought more fully in the section on unity of command.

VISION

Where there is no vision [no redemptive revelation of God], the people perish.

—PROVERBS 29:18

The mission describes why the special ops church exists, while the vision is more descriptive as to where special ops Christians are headed.

The vision of Angel Fire Christian Center is expressed in this statement:

We are Angel Fire Christian Center, a special ops church made up of highly motivated special ops Christians dedicated to fulfilling the Great Commission by discipling nations.

We serve the body of Christ as a special ops church that produces and sends special ops Christians to the nations imbued with the highest ideals of Christian love and friendship.

We teach teamwork to special ops Christians through a fully integrated curriculum of tactical/strategic training and practical biblical studies designed to release people in their individual responsibilities within the structure of team ministry.

We challenge people to achieve their full potential in spirit, soul, and body. We provide a comprehensive support system to ensure individual growth and success.

We value the cultural and ethnic diversity of the people and nations we serve. We are dedicated to winning their hearts and minds by the love of Jesus Christ.

We, the warriors of the special ops Christian team, recognize Jesus Christ as the chief Cornerstone of our reputation for excellence. We take pride in sending the highest quality of special ops Christians to disciple the nations.

CODE OF CONDUCT

The codes of conduct are principles that guide our behavior on the journey to the vision. The following principles of accountability, loyalty, integrity, and teamwork make up the code of conduct for the special ops church and the special ops Christian.

Accountability

Special Ops Christians are committed to accountability for process improvement and individual quality performance.

Special ops churches are not a place for outlaw, lone wolf, and Rambo-type Christians. When I first arrived in Vietnam I inherited a very experienced recon team. I am sorry to say that they were a bunch of do-your-own-thing characters who refused to be accountable. They would disregard the mission and were notorious for big shootouts with the enemy. Their platoon leader and a fine lieutenant had been killed three months before I arrived, and without an officer to be accountable to, these young marines had become a danger to themselves and the integrity of the entire unit. Their patrols rarely lasted the five days required to complete the mission.

I ran two patrols with this team. Due to their ineptness, two of them were seriously wounded. They refused to be accountable and they suffered for it. My commanding officer questioned me about the team's performance in the field. I was honest and told him they were undisciplined. I asked him specifically to give me new, inexperienced marines to work with. I taught the new crop of recon marines the importance of accountability, and we had a highly successful year. There is no room for chronically rebellious people in a special ops church. It takes a disciple, not just a convert, to complete the mission Jesus Christ has given us to complete.

Loyalty

> We the special ops church are dedicated to the highest principles of interpersonal and organizational trust, honor, and loyalty while maintaining ethical conduct.

Loyalty is everything when it comes to the special ops church. Jesus valued loyalty. Peter, through repentance for his disloyalty, was forgiven by the Lord, as recorded in John 21:15–17. Not every form of disloyalty should be characterized as that of Judas. Loyalty to Christ, along with loyalty to interpersonal as well organizational relationships, must be lived out among special ops Christians. I have heard believers say, "My loyalty is to Christ and Him alone." That may sound good on the surface, but I have heard this from some of the most rebellious believers I have ever met. They violate the Lord's chain of command

and often try to serve as self-appointed five-fold ministers in the body of Christ. They often try to draw disciples away after themselves. Jesus called for loyalty in John 6:52–59:

> Then the Jews began to argue sharply among themselves, "How can this man give us his flesh to eat?" Jesus said to them, "I tell you the truth, unless you eat the flesh of the Son of Man and drink his blood; you have no life in you. Whoever eats my flesh and drinks my blood has eternal life, and I will raise him up at the last day. For my flesh is real food and my blood is real drink. Whoever eats my flesh and drinks my blood remains in me, and I in him. Just as the living Father sent me and I live because of the Father, so the one who feeds on me will live because of me. This is the bread that came down from heaven. Your forefathers ate manna and died, but he who feeds on this bread will live forever." He said this while teaching in the synagogue in Capernaum. (NIV)

Just a few verses later in John 6:66–67 it says, "From this time many of his disciples turned back and no longer followed him. 'You do not want to leave too, do you?' Jesus asked the Twelve" (NIV). This is the question that Jesus is posing to His Church today—"You do not want to leave too, do you?" We must eat the whole loaf if we are to be effective Christians in this current season. A true disciple or special ops Christian does not pick out the pieces of Christ that satisfy him, but he eats the whole loaf of the bread that has come down from heaven.

More on Loyalty

Upon joining the Special Ops Force Recon unit in March 1969, I was introduced to five other lieutenants who would become my life-long friends. Such loyalty I have never found in the contemporary church. We ran missions together and stayed up all night monitoring each other's patrols on the radio when one of us was surrounded by the enemy. We wept and laughed together. Trust, honor, and loyalty were expected at all times in our relationship. Our careers and competi-

41

tiveness took a backseat to our all-important brotherhood. Over the course of the year, we built interpersonal relationships that prove to be second to none decades later.

"One for all and all for one" was more than just a phrase in our life together in war. I remember taking a North Vietnamese soldier prisoner, when suddenly three other heavily armed North Vietnamese soldiers confronted me. Lt. Wayne Rollings, one of the five lieutenants, stepped between the enemy and me and cut them down with a blast of automatic rifle fire. Wayne retired from the Marine Corps a few years ago as a major general. He now serves on the advisory board of the International Children's Aid Network, our non-profit organization that builds Children's Villages.

Warriors are not likely to be the type of people to simply exchange birthday cards. The relationship goes much deeper. It is the call to close ranks and run toward the battle that separates a true warrior from a wannabe warrior. Organizational or church loyalty, I believe, grows out of interpersonal loyalty. Jesus said, "Greater love has no man than this, that a man lay down his life for his friends" (John 15:13). There is no room for so-called corporate climbers in the special ops church. Corporate climbers are those who step on the backs of their contemporaries on the way to privileged positions in an organization.

Ethical conduct is protected in our pursuit of true loyalty by "speaking the truth in love" (Eph. 4:15). When our motive is based on love, our conduct will be ethical, not marked by self-serving disloyalty.

Integrity

> We are committed to integrity in all our actions, words, and deeds. Only through the courage of our convictions, tempered with a sense of personal honor, humility, and ethical behavior, can we achieve our goals in Jesus Christ.

Integrity is defined as "soundness, or the adherence to a code of values." It is utter sincerity, honesty, candor, and completeness.[3] Someone once said that if you don't stand for something, you will fall for everything. Many Christians today change churches like they change their underwear. Special ops Christians should value relationships in the church. When they commit to a relationship, they should be candid in that relationship. They don't have to agree with everything that happens in the organization; they just need to show some integrity. When a disciple is trapped in a church that is not involved with the Great Commission, they simply need to be properly released after respectfully making their case.

I remember when things weren't going well for our Force Recon teams in the spring of 1969 in Vietnam. Our teams were getting shot out of landing zones deep in enemy-controlled territory because our adversary had caught on to how we came into a landing zone. It was nearly impossible trying to set a chopper down in a hot landing zone while the enemy raked the team with automatic weapon fire. I remember Lieutenant Ric Miller was shot out of six of these landing zones in one day. Ric even had his jungle cover (hat) shot off his head. Rather than the six of us lieutenants rebelling and wanting to leave, we talked over the insertion procedure of the helicopters that were delivering our teams into hostile landing zones. Then we respectfully lobbied for some changes. The air wing stopped prepping the zones with air strikes and quickly went straight into the landing zone undetected. We would get off quickly and start our mission before the enemy could react. Integrity, honesty, candor, and the courage of our convictions caused us to enjoy great success as individuals and as an organization.[4]

Teamwork

We are committed to the principles of teamwork, selfless service, professionalism, mutual respect, trust, along with free and open communications. We value a concern for the individual and an appreciation for cultural and gender diversity.

A team is a number of persons associated in work or activity. It is a group on one side in a competitive contest.[5] A good team works together, and that makes for good teamwork.

On April 12, 1969, I witnessed teamwork operate in an eight-man recon team that was badly outnumbered in a battle with enemy forces on the border between Vietnam and Loas. The team exemplified selfless service, professionalism, mutual respect and trust as they fought to save each other in a desperate battle. That day I witnessed clear concern for individual marines with total appreciation for cultural diversity. That day in 1969 Marine Force Recon team, call sign Recline, was inserted onto Hill 551 in the central highlands of South Vietnam. Waiting for the eight-man recon team were several hundred well-armed enemy soldiers. The helicopter was struck over thirty times as the team disembarked and barely could fly off the hill. The team took cover in a bomb crater and for the next three and a half hours the marines had to fend off an attack from hundreds of determined North Vietnamese soldiers. I was assistant patrol leader on the mission and can say unequivocally that without teamwork, our small recon unit would have been wiped out. We had to work together communicating with one another where to fire our weapons, throw grenades, and launch rocket-propelled grenades. Our team leader, Ric Miller, had to help direct helicopter gunship fire and Phantom Jet napalm and bombing runs within thirty meters of our position. I crawled around the bomb crater on my knees and fired over one hundred high explosive rounds from an M-79 grenade launcher. Everybody had a job that day, and each member of the team was called upon to be selfless and professional. Free and open communication flowed between the eight of us as we hollered orders back and forth across the bomb crater.

At one point our air support warned us that two hundred enemy soldiers were approaching our position using a blind spot we had in our defensive perimeter. We beat back their attack just before they reached the lip of the bomb crater. The crater was the only protection we had from the enemy's automatic weapon fire. Cultural diversity wasn't an issue as a Latino; Private Castro, PFC. Jones, and Corporal Taylor, who were African American; and five Caucasians, two of them from the deep South, worked as a team. Finally, another helicopter pilot braved the withering fire and landed his craft. He waited until our whole team was aboard and then lifted off the hill as enemy fire tore holes in the helicopter's thin shell. The pilot's name was Lt. William G. Peters. Yes, he and I shared the same first and last name. Even after an enemy bullet had shattered the glass in the cockpit of his helicopter, Peters kept the craft on the ground until every member of our recon team had boarded. The Marine Corps promotes the concept of the ground/air team. Its importance is ingrained in the infantry and air units.

Lt. Peters died two months after pulling us off Hill 551. He crashed his helicopter trying to rescue another recon team. He received the nation's second highest combat award, the Navy Cross, for service above and beyond the call of duty and for his selfless action in getting our team off Hill 551.[6]

Teamwork can mean everything as special ops Christians brave the uncertainties of traveling into unsafe neighborhoods at home and equally perilous regions abroad. A good team works together. The special ops church must respect this part of the code of conduct and come up to a higher standard than has been manifested by the contemporary church. How many church splits have occurred because members could not work as a team while they tried to perform the most routine tasks, like changing the décor of the sanctuary?

The Nine Principles of War

The nine principles of war are the rules of conduct that guide our judgment on the journey toward fulfilling our mission and vision. A principle, according to Merriam-Webster's Dictionary, is a rule of conduct.[7]

The following are the nine principles of war:

1. unity of command
2. objective
3. offensive
4. mass-power
5. economy of force
6. maneuver
7. security
8. surprise
9. simplicity[8]

I first learned these war-fighting principles at Marine Corps Officers Candidate School, Quantico, Virginia, in the summer of 1967. While the hippies had their Summer of Love in San Francisco, nine hundred of us patriots were trying out to become marine officers in a ten-week boot camp. Four hundred and fifty of us graduated from the course and became second lieutenants. I reported to O.C.S. weighing two hundred pounds and graduated a lean 172 pounds. One of the things the drill instructors pounded into us was the nine principles of war. At that time they taught us the acronym MOOSEMUSS: mission, objective, offensive, security, execution, unity of command, surprise, and simplicity. I have taken the liberty to define and modify some of these to reflect some of the experiences I have had in ministry over the years.

These guides to judgment known worldwide as the principles of war need to serve as rules of conduct for the special ops church. These principles of war, with variations, have been tried and tested over the centuries by armies of many nations. They have been developed out of thousands of years of military conflicts worldwide. When nations and their warriors have obeyed these principles, they have had great success. When these principles have been ignored or violated, mighty nations have suffered great defeat on the battlefield. World War II and Desert Storm are examples of victory when the United States of America obeyed the principles of war. The Vietnam War is an example of the great loss a nation suffers when these principles are violated. When they are adhered to, these principles become proven guides to sound judgments that ultimately lead to victory in battle.

Spiritual warfare has much in common with natural warfare. The most common trait between spiritual and natural warfare is that the lives and futures of people are at stake. Although the principles of war were developed for natural conflict, it is evident they also can easily apply to spiritual conflict.

> For we are not wrestling with flesh and blood [contending only with physical opponents], but against the despotisms, against powers, against [the master spirits who are] the world rulers of this present darkness, against the spirit forces of wickedness in the heavenly (supernatural) sphere.
> —EPHESIANS 6:12, AMP

DEFINITIONS OF THE NINE PRINCIPLES OF WAR

- **Unity of Command:** the unity of effort under one responsible leader, or cooperation among multiple leaders
- **Objective:** a direct vision toward attainable goals in a good plan of action
- **Offensive:** the act of aggressively seizing, retaining, and exploiting momentum and initiative in battle
- **Mass-Power:** the release of your force in the most effective time, place, and manner to overwhelm the opposition

- **Economy of Force:** effective use of your force that overwhelms the opposition while preserving your resources
- **Maneuver:** the mobility and flexibility of your force in your effort to achieve your objective
- **Security:** the protection of everything vital to the accomplishment of your objectives
- **Surprise:** the launch of an offensive against the opposition, in a place and manner that they are unprepared for, at an unexpected time
- **Simplicity:** the organization of plans, as well as communication of orders, in simple, clear, and concise manner[9]

In Chapter 8 we will discuss the special ops Christian and the church's weapon of choice, which is the Word of God. In the following chapters we will use the code of conduct, rules of conduct, and the nine principles of war, to develop the mission and vision of the special ops church. By way of review, the mission defines the reason for the special ops church's existence. The vision describes where special ops Christians are headed. The guiding principles of the code of conduct and rules of conduct—the Nine Principles of War—guide the special ops Christian's behavior and judgment on the journey to fulfilling the mission and vision of the special ops church.

CHAPTER 4

UNITY OF COMMAND

APRIL 25, 1969—AN HOA, SOUTH VIETNAM

Six Marine Corps lieutenants and team leaders of the most elite unit in the Corps gather in their tent for a very serious meeting with their First Force Reconnaissance Company commanding officer. The month of April wasn't over and already they experienced the death of two helicopter pilots, one recon Marine killed, and a dozen wounded. Through small arms, artillery, and air strikes their recon teams had killed hundreds of the enemy. In spite of the success, these lieutenants realized the enemy was aware of their tactics and that soon the casualty rate among their recon teams was going to dramatically increase.

Rain began to pound the tent as the commanding officer and his executive officer entered through the drawn flap. The meeting would be short and to the point. The lieutenants wanted air strikes on helicopter landing zones stopped prior to the insert of their teams. They also were asking for better air support in the way of emergency extractions under fire. The lieutenants were asking their commanding officer to trust them and their judgment when under fire. They felt they had proved their commitment to the mission of First Force Recon by risking their lives above and beyond the call of duty over the past few months, and they were right.

The company commander, a major, was an experienced leader and recon marine. Just a few years earlier he had placed number one at the British Commando School in the U.K. This commando school, along with the Israeli commando training, was considered the best in the world at the time. He realized at that moment of candid confrontation with his officer corps that his unity of command was on the line. Rather than shatter his lieutenants' trust in his leadership by rebuffing them, he patiently listened to their concerns. He then agreed to change some of the company's standard operating procedures to better serve the teams in the field. With a stroke of brilliant leadership our commanding officer had gathered the unwavering support of his team leaders and secured the success of his company for the duration of its mission in Vietnam.[1]

Because the principle of war known as unity of command was adhered to, the company went on to win battle after battle with very light casualties. Not only was the unity of effort under one responsible leader secured, but the cooperation of his subordinate officers was also secured. *Courageous* is the best word for the integrity displayed by the lieutenants in speaking up, and *brilliant* is the best word for the company commander's response.

UNITY OF COMMAND

War requires unity of effort under one responsible leader or cooperation among multiple leaders.

Unity of command is one of the nine principles of war every nation's military uses as a guide to judge an organization's pursuit of its mission. History has proven if you violate any of the nine principles of war for any length of time, you dramatically increase your chances of losing the war.

A lack of unity of command occurs when various levels of leadership in an organization frustrates cooperation or unity of effort in the pursuit of its mission and vision. If leadership in the special ops church does not have unity of command, it will fail to become an effective force in the discipling of nations. We have already established in this book that we are in a spiritual war with powers of darkness. Violation of the principles of war can bring a resounding defeat to the special ops church. Defeat of the church means special ops Christians will also experience personal loss at the hands of the enemy.

First, special ops Christians must strive for a unity of command in their own spiritual lives. They must take their lead from the Holy Spirit and not from the flesh. They must strive for a unity of command in their marriages, businesses, and ministries. It is not enough for a special ops Christian to be supportive of the unity of command in the church while their personal lives are falling apart. Once again, their relationship with the Head, Jesus Christ, is a key to victory.

The strength of the special ops church is the special ops Christian, and the strength of the special ops Christian is the special ops church.

The decisive application of mass, full combat power requires unity of command. The special ops church attains unity of effort by the coordinated action of all forces toward a common mission and vision. Although coordination may be attained by cooperation, it is best achieved by vesting a single commander with the requisite authority. If you try to run a special ops church by committee, you will fail. Somebody must be responsible to steer the ship of ministry, and more than one set of hands on the wheel at a time can spell disaster. Unity of command is designed to facilitate attainment of the mission and vision.

Tactical Level: Day to day battle in the trenches.

Strategic Level: The "big picture" level involves political and military coordination.

In South Africa, I have delegated my authority at the tactical level of operations in our special ops coalition to a South African apostle. He is responsible for building four Children's Villages. I understand that a commander in the field close to the battle best makes day-to-day tactical decisions. I have vested the authority to a single commander who lives in Soweto and understands building in Africa better than I do. As the visionary apostle, I must retain unity of command at the strategic level, known as the big picture level, to help integrate key political and military objectives. Nevertheless, I must remember that at the tactical level there must also be unity of command if we are expected to win our daily battles. Trying to hold all authority at the strategic level will eventually choke the victory at the tactical level. Some authority must be delegated. All building would cease if I tried to make day-to-day tactical decisions about South Africa from the States. Part of our job in the Great Commission is to find competent resident apostles and prophets to carry the battle to the enemy in their region. Our job is to help empower them for the completion of the mission/vision we share with these leaders. Economic empowerment is merely sharing the wealth of our church with projects that impact the kingdom of God.

The mission and vision of the special ops church must be fully in line with the political objectives of the kingdom of God. The main political objective of the kingdom of God is to disciple nations. Unity of command of the special ops church is best vested in an apostle or prophet that understands the political objective as well as the battlefield mission. If not combined in one apostle, then the battlefield commander should be a part of the lead apostle or prophet's cabinet of leadership.

THE FATHER, SON, AND HOLY SPIRIT HAVE PERFECT UNITY OF COMMAND

The Godhead (the Trinity) is the ultimate manifestation of the principle of unity of command. In the war with Satan, the Godhead agreed on the strategic objective to redeem mankind.

1. The Father sent the Son to Earth.
2. The Son agreed with the Father and Holy Spirit and kept the power of the perfect unity of command.

3. The Son returned to the Father.

4. The Holy Spirit was then sent to the earth in agreement with the Father and Son.

Special ops Christians must be familiar with the history of the structure of spiritual authority in the earth, which stems from Adam to Jesus Christ.

It will be beneficial at this point to review the problems the sinful fall of man created among God, man, and Satan. Between Genesis 1:1 and Genesis 1:2, Satan's high act of treason results in the devil being cast down to Earth. In the process, Satan brought his iniquity from heaven to Earth. God created the earth from the void, and then restored the earth. God created man, Adam, and gave him dominion and seed. (See Genesis 1:26–29.) God created the woman, Eve, and Satan deceived her. Adam was not initially deceived, but he later joined Satan and committed high treason, causing man to go astray.

> All we like sheep have gone astray; we have turned every one to his own way; and the LORD hath laid on him the iniquity of us all.
>
> —ISAIAH 53:6

Isaiah 53:6 speaks of God, order, and authority, but Satan didn't get it. Satan has had to piggyback on man's limited authority. He has had to usurp authority. God continues to this very day to exercise His authority through His Son, Jesus Christ.

> God, who at sundry times and in diverse manners spake in time past unto the fathers by the prophets, Hath in these last days spoken unto us by his Son.
>
> —HEBREWS 1:1–2

Romans 5:14 says Adam was a type of Christ. There had to be a second Adam or a second Christ, "the Anointed," to bring to fruition God's full intention for man and the earth. God found another way to get His covenant back into the earth through a man named Abram. (See Genesis 17:1–7.) Abram was chosen because God knew Abram would command his family to follow him.

Christians relate to three Old Testament men in the following manner.

- Adam we relate to racially.
- Abraham we relate to through covenant.
- David we relate to royally.

Jesus related to Adam, Abraham, and David in the following way.

- References to Jesus in the Gospels refer to Him as the Son of David, not Son of Adam or Son of Abraham.
- In Matthew 1, Jesus is spoken of as "Son of Abraham and Son of David."
- Jesus related to David because He would be the final royal King or the finalization of God's redemptive purpose.

The Father, Son, and Holy Spirit defeated Satan with the first strategic objective, redeeming mankind by sending Jesus, who accomplished victory on the cross. "He was made sin for us who knew no sin, that we might be made the righteousness of God in Him," according to 2 Corinthians 5:21. In Ephesians 4:8–10 Paul says, "Wherefore he saith, When he ascended up on high, he led captivity captive, and gave gifts unto men. (Now that he ascended, what is it but that he also descended first into the lower parts of the earth? He that descended is the same also that ascended up far above all heavens, that he might fill all things.)" Satan was compelled by the resurrection power of Jesus to give up the captives in the para-dise section of Hades, men who in righteousness like Moses, Jacob, Isaiah, and David began their ascension with Jesus. The Greek word *aichmalosia* means "captivity." *Vine's Expository Dictionary of New Testament Words* suggests that at His ascension, Christ transferred the redeemed Old Testament saints from Sheol to His own presence in glory.² Those righteously judged for having rejected God's counsel under the old economy were left in hell.

Then these Old Testament saints continued up and up to the ramparts of glory, where they shouted, "Lift up your heads, O ye gates; and be ye lift up, ye everlasting doors; and the King of glory shall come in." The mighty angels shouted back, "Who is this King of glory?" The saints shouted back, "The LORD strong and mighty, the LORD mighty in battle. Lift up your heads, O ye gates; even lift them up, ye everlasting doors; and the King of glory shall come in." The angel once again challenged, "Who is this King of glory?" The saints shouted, "The LORD of hosts, he is the King of glory" (Ps. 24:7–10). Then the second strategic objective was brought forward that would make Jesus' enemies His footstool.

> For David did not ascend to heaven, and yet he said, "The Lord said to my Lord: Sit at my right hand until I make your enemies a footstool for your feet." Therefore let all Israel be assured of this: God has made this Jesus, whom you cruci-fied, both Lord and Christ.
>
> —ACTS 2:34–36, NIV

Before the commanding officer of a unit rotates to a new duty station in the military, there is a change of command ceremony. The ceremony is performed publicly, and the new command structure is given authority, replacing the old command. In a divine change of command ceremony, Jesus ascended to the right hand of His Father and was seated on His throne as King. He sent the Holy Spirit to replace Him on Earth and gave gifts to men to rule his church. The old covenant was being replaced by a new command structure for a new covenant.

During the Ascension, Jesus left gifts to men. In Ephesians 4:11 Paul says, "And His *gifts* were [varied; He Himself appointed and gave men to us] some to be apostles (special messengers) some prophets (inspired preachers and expounders), some evangelists (preachers of the Gospel, traveling missionaries), some pastors (shepherds of the flock) and teachers" (AMP, emphasis added). The operative word is *gift*.

In the old covenant, the word *gift* in reference to authority appears in Numbers 18:6-7: "And I, behold, have taken your brethren the Levites from among the children of Israel: to you they are given as a *gift* for the LORD, to do the service of the tabernacle of the congregation. Therefore thou and thy sons with thee shall keep your priest's office for everything of the altar, and within the veil; and ye shall serve: I have given your priest's office unto you as a service of *gift*" (emphasis added).

When the curtain in the temple separating the people from the holy of holies was ripped from top to bottom, the Aaronic priesthood was no longer needed. The Levitical priesthood or gift was no longer needed because a new command or new covenant was activated. The new gift for the new command structure is found in Ephesians 4:11, beginning with the apostle and prophet.

Unity of Command in the Special Ops Church

The apostle and prophet in the command structure of the special ops church

The definition, function, and characteristics of an apostle:
Our English word is a transliteration of the Greek *apostolos*, which is derived from *apostellein*, "to send." Whereas several words for "send" are used in the New Testament, expressing such ideas as "dispatch," "release," or "dismiss," *apostellein* emphasizes the elements of commission—authority of and responsibility to the sender. So an apostle is properly one sent on a definite mission, in which he acts with full authority on behalf of the sender and is accountable to him.[3]

Naomi Dowdy, a commissioned apostle with a huge Asian sphere of influence, gives us better understanding of the meaning of the name "apostle" as it was used during the time of the Roman Empire in her book Commissioning. Naomi tells us that in Jesus' days, apostles were chosen military generals who were sent out as official emissaries from a government or an empire to conquer a new territory. She goes on to say that one of the assigned responsibilities after conquering a territory was to teach the conquered people the language, customs, values, and ways of the new kingdom of which they had become a part.[4] These military apostolic responsibilities seem to fall right in line with the Great Commission of Jesus Christ to go and make disciples of the nations.

Apostles function in the following ways:

- plant churches and open up new regions to the gospel,
- bring order and strength to existing churches,
- consistently reveal and restore truth to the church, and
- dismantle worthless tradition and religious ritual in the church.

Characteristics of an apostle are:

- humble, servant like attitude;
- preaches the kingdom of God with miracles, signs, and wonders;
- sacrificial and long-suffering service;
- power and authority in preaching the Word; and
- a relationship with Christ through a powerful personal revelation.

Unity of command in the special ops church begins with vesting unity of effort under the authority of the apostle with the cooperation of other five-fold ministers and church leaders.

The role of the apostle in the command structure of the modern church, especially the special ops church, is extremely important to understand. This subject can be polarizing, but it is time we deal with it. The first point I would like to make is that there is no scriptural basis for declaring that the ministries of apostle and prophet were ever meant to be temporary. Like the charismatic gifts in 1 Corinthians 12–14, the offices of apostle and prophet (Eph. 4:11), probably went into decline because men lost sight of Christ's intention within the first four centuries of the church. However after about a fifteen hundred-year decline, the charismatic gifts and the ministry gifts of apostle and prophet have been restored over the last century.

The special ops church cannot fulfill its mission or vision using the democratic form of command found in many denominations. The major problem of the democratic forms of government within denominations is they defy the New Testament model for the recognition of apostle and prophets.

Apostles and prophets assume authority in the command structure of the special ops Church under the sovereign appointment of the Lord, however their leadership and influence is often intimidating to the paradigm of the conventional church. Apostolic gifts are often bound by the function of the bureaucracy of most conventional churches. Administrators often rule the church and bind the spiritual activity of the apostle and prophet. Rather than the sovereign election of apostles and prophets by God, churches have opted for human appointments.

Prophets are inspired preachers, expounders, inspired interpreters of the will and purposes of God, and anointed teachers, according to the Amplified Bible. (See Ephesians 4:11.) Chuck Pierce writes in his book *Interpreting the Times*, "Intercessors stand, Prophets decree, and Apostles execute."[5] We will read in later chapters about the execution phase of a battle plan. The absence of the apostle during the execution phase of a spiritual battle would be like not having General George Patton involved in the battle for North Africa in World War II. The absence of our apostles of heavy weight in certain spiritual battles would be like General Eisenhower sidelined during D-Day. The truth is that apostles in the contemporary church have been excluded from the planning and execution phase of key spiritual battles over strategic territories across the face of the earth.

Paul describes the plight of the apostle in 2 Corinthians 6:3–10:

We put no obstruction in anybody's way [we give no offense in anything], so that no fault may be found and [our] ministry blamed and discredited. But we commend ourselves in every way as [true] servants of God: through great endurance, in tribulation and suffering, in hardships and privations, in sore straits and calamities, In beatings, imprisonments, riots, labors, sleepless watching, hunger; By innocence and purity, knowledge and spiritual insight, longsuffering and patience, kindness, in the Holy Spirit, in unfeigned love; By [speaking] the word of truth, in the power of God, with the weapons of righteousness for the right hand [to attack] and for the left hand [to defend]; Amid honor and dishonor; in defaming and evil report and in praise and good report. [We are branded]as deceivers [impostors] and [yet vindicated as] truthful and honest. [We are treated] as unknown and ignored [by God and His people]; as dying, and yet here we are alive; as chastened by suffering and [yet] not killed; As grieved and mourning, yet [we are] always rejoicing; as poor, [ourselves, yet] bestowing riches on many; as having nothing, and [yet in reality] possessing all things. (AMP)

It is not my intention to fully define the office of prophet in this book. Some say the office of the prophet was fully released back to the body of Christ about 1988 and the office of the apostle was fully released about 1998. Apostles are a vital part of the execution phase of God's end-time plans for His kingdom. Church history reveals that the five-fold ministry as shared in Ephesians 4:11 disappeared from the church by the fifth century and has been slowly restored in the last one hundred years. With this understanding, it is much easier to understand God's plan for restoring His anointed gifts to the church. Many good books have been written about the office of the prophet but few have been published on the ministry of the apostle.

THE AUTHORITY OF THE APOSTLE
OVER THE SPECIAL OPS CHURCH

The word *apostle* appears nine times in the Gospels, thirty times in Acts, thirty-nine times in the Epistles, and three times in the Book of Revelation.

New apostles besides the original apostles of the Lamb are mentioned in the New Testament to include:

1. Mathias—"And they drew lots [between the two], and the lot fell on Mathias; and he was added to and counted with the eleven apostles (special messengers)" (Acts 1:26, AMP).

2. Paul—"Paul, summoned by the will and purpose of God to be an apostle (special messenger) of Christ Jesus, and our brother Sosthenes" (1 Cor. 1:1, AMP).

3. Barnabas—"But when the apostles Barnabas and Paul heard of it; they tore their clothing and dashed out among the crowd, shouting" (AMP).

4. Andronicus and Junias: "Remember me to Andronicus and Junias, my tribal kinsmen and once my fellow prisoners. They are men held in high esteem among the apostles, who also were in Christ before I was" (Rom. 16:7, AMP).

5. James—"But I did not see any of the other apostles (the special messengers of Christ) except James the brother of our Lord" (Gal. 1:19, AMP).

6. Titus—"For this reason I left you [behind] in Crete, that you might set right what was defective and finish what was left undone, and that you might appoint elders and set them over the churches (assemblies) in every city as I directed you" (Titus 1:5, AMP).

7. Epaphroditus—"However, I thought it necessary to send Epaphroditus [back] to you. [He has been] my brother and companion in labor and my fellow soldier, as well as

[having come as] your special messenger (apostle) and minister to my need" (Phil. 2:25, AMP).

8. Silas and Timothy—"Paul, Silvanus (Silas), and Timothy, to the assembly (church) of the Thessalonians in God the Father and the Lord Jesus Christ (the Messiah): Grace (spiritual blessing and divine favor) to you and [heart] peace.... Nor did we seek to extract praise and honor and glory from men, either from you or from any one else, though we might have asserted our authority [stood on our dignity and claimed honor] as apostles (special missionaries) of Christ (the Messiah)" (Thess. 1:1; 2:6, AMP).

9. Apollos—"Now I have applied all this [about parties and factions] to myself and Apollos.... For it seems to me that God has made an exhibit of us apostles, exposing us to view last [of all, like men in a triumphal procession who are] sentenced to death [and displayed at the end of the line]" (1 Cor. 4:6, 9, AMP).

The special ops church cannot ignore the appointed and anointed apostolic office given by the Lord Jesus Christ as a gift to the church. The apostolic ministry closely resembles the sending of Jesus by the Father. Jesus said, "As my Father hath sent me, even so send I you" (John 20:21). The apostle is sent with the same authority, with a unique equipping of authority and gifting to plant churches, set them in divine order, and provide them with godly leadership and direction. Apostolic leaders impart anointed vision and faith. The special ops church receives great favor and blessing from God by honoring apostolic leadership.

As previously stated, the offices of apostle, prophet, evangelist, pastor, and teacher are known as the five-fold ministry. Once again, their reason for existing is clearly stated in Ephesians 4:12. In that verse, Paul wrote that Jesus' "intention was the perfecting and the full equipping of the saints (His consecrated people), [that they should do] the work of ministering toward building up Christ's body (the church)" (AMP).

The spiritual authority of the apostle within the command structure of the special ops church and apostolic center is very broad.

- Apostles teach—"I teach every where in every church" (1 Cor. 4:17)
- Apostles ordain—"Ordain I in all the churches" (1 Cor. 7:17)
- Apostles discipline—"If any man obey not our word" (2 Thess. 3:14)
- Apostles structure—"The rest will I set in order when I come" (1 Cor. 11:34).
- Apostles judge—"I...have judged already" (1 Cor. 5:3).
- Apostles oversee—"Care of all the churches" (2 Cor. 11:28)

So God appointed some in the church [for His own use]: first apostles (special messengers); second prophets (inspired preachers and expounders); third teachers; then wonder-workers; then those with the ability to heal the sick; helpers; administrators; [speakers in] different (unknown) tongues.

—1 CORINTHIANS 12:28, AMP

The church in general must receive the appointed apostolic leadership of the Lord and build its unity of command around it. Church constitutions or legislation is not what establishes apostolic unity of command. It is established by divine appointment and recognized by other apostles and the anointed church structures. Its sphere of influence can be local, regional, national, and international.

APOSTOLIC CENTERS ARE CHURCHES OVERSEEN BY APOSTLES, PROPHETS, AND ELDERS

Apostolic centers are churches where apostles, prophets, and other five-fold ministry gifts are in abundance. They are places of training as well as places where doctrine is discussed, and through the inspiration of the Holy Spirit, strategic plans are drawn up for the advancement of the kingdom of God in the earth. Jerusalem, Antioch, and Ephesus were all apostolic centers in the early church.

> But some men came down from Judea and were instructing the brethren, Unless you are circumcised in accordance with the Mosaic custom, you cannot be saved. And when Paul and Barnabas had no small disagreement and discussion with them, it was decided that Paul and Barnabas and some of the other of their number should go up Jerusalem [and confer] with the apostles (special messengers) and the elders about this matter.
>
> —Acts 15:1–2, AMP

In the past, men have tried to work out of a local church mentality where five-fold ministry was not recognized and often quenched. Apostolic centers can give birth to new apostolic special ops churches and new apostolic centers. Often apostolic companies made up of a team of five-fold ministers and believers with other giftings will be sent to establish these new expressions of church.

> Now in the church (assembly) at Antioch there were prophets (inspired interpreters of the will and purposes of God) and teachers: Barnabas, Symeon who was called Niger [Black], Lucius of Cyrene, Manaen a member of the court of Herod the tetrarch, and Saul. While they were worshiping the Lord and fasting, the Holy Spirit said, Separate now Me Barnabas and Saul for the work to which I have called them. Then after fasting and praying, they put their hands on them and sent them away. So then, being sent out by the Holy Spirit, they went down to Seleucia, and from [that port] sailed away to Cyprus.
>
> —Acts 13:1–4, AMP

Apostolic centers arise where God begins to do a strategic work in a given territory. Apostolic centers can be likened to military command

63

centers. Each command center in the military is set up to best serve the accomplishment of the mission and overall objective of the battle. The gifts gathered around an apostolic center will ultimately define its main purpose in God's grand strategic objective. The Marine Corps is generally organized around squads of six men, platoons (thirty men), companies (250 men), battalions (one thousand men), regiments (four thousand men), and divisions (twelve thousand men). In this configuration of personnel, there are command centers set up for communications, logistics, motor transport, air support, artillery, intelligence, and operations, among others.

I say all of this to say that you cannot cookie-cut apostolic centers. They will differ in purpose and mission according to the sovereign will of God. It will take the Holy Spirit to get the centers into perfect unity of command in the years ahead. With men, this kind of unity of purpose seems impossible, but "with God all things are possible" (Matt. 19:26).

SUMMARY

This is a list of a few characteristics of an apostolic center:

- There are apostles, prophets, and elders governing the apostolic center.
- The offices of evangelist, pastor, and teacher are resident in the center.
- There are intercessors, miracle workers, and seer ministries resident.
- There is a Bible school and training curriculum administered by five-fold mentors and teachers.
- There is apostolic strategic and tactical planning for the Great Commission operations worldwide.
- Disciples involved in the apostolic center perform signs and wonders every day.
- Ministers are sent by the guidance of the Holy Spirit to strategic territories all over the earth.

- Apostles of commerce (business people) are resident in an apostolic center.
- Financing the kingdom of God is the priority of every apostolic center, and wealthy centers share with the less fortunate centers.

Remember, unity of command is one of the nine principles of war. If any of the principles of war are violated for a significant amount of time, the violators are in grave danger of losing the entire war. While recovering unity of command, there is the danger of losing key battles in whatever theater of war the church is presently engaged.

CHAPTER 5

THE OBJECTIVE

THE PRINCIPLES OF war call for one grand strategic objective. It is common military knowledge that after the Vietnam War several military study groups discovered there were more than twenty grand strategic objectives guiding that war.[1] No matter how many goals and good action plans the U.S. had, the military was doomed to fail because it had no clear grand strategic objective.

Likewise, the special ops church must not take lightly its grand strategic objective, which is to fulfill the Great Commission and usher in the rule and authority of the kingdom of God in the earth. The church as a whole has not really taken ownership of either objective. The church often resembles secular organizations that make a lot of noise about making Earth a better place but never really get it out of committee.

THE CORPORATE SPECIAL OPS CHURCH AND ITS OBJECTIVE

Objective: a direct vision toward attainable goals in a good plan of action[2]

As previously stated, the special ops churches' mission and vision must lead to the grand strategic objective of Jesus Christ, the Head of the church. The grand strategic objective is the key objective that will satisfy the political reason the war is being fought. In Matthew 28:18–20 Jesus reveals His grand strategic objective:

Jesus approached and, breaking the silence, said to them, All authority (all power of rule) in heaven and on earth has been given to Me. Go then and make disciples of all the nations, baptizing them into the name of the Father and of the Son and of the Holy Spirit, Teaching them to observe everything that I have commanded you, and behold, I am with you all the days (perpetually, uniformly, and on every occasion), to the [very] close and consummation of the age. (AMP)

The mission of the special ops church must compliment the grand strategic objective of our Commander in Chief, Jesus Christ. We judge the mission of the special ops church on whether or not its mission feeds into His grand strategic objective. Remember, the mission is the reason why the special ops church exists.

The mission of the special ops church is to develop people from every nation morally and physically and to imbue them with an unconditional love for mankind, found in the triune God (Father, Son, and Holy Spirit)…[and] to engender in people's character the highest responsibilities of the kingdom of God in command, citizenship, and government throughout the nations.[3]

The mission statement is clearly supportive of the grand strategic objective of discipling nations for Jesus Christ. Phrases such as "to develop people from every nation morally and physically and to imbue them with an unconditional love for mankind, found in the triune God" speak for themselves.

Now let's turn toward the vision of the special ops church and see how it lines up with the grand strategic objective of Jesus Christ. The vision describes where the special ops church is headed. The vision of the special ops church states:

We are the special ops church, made up of highly motivated special ops Christians dedicated to fulfilling the
Great Commission while ushering in the kingdom of God.
We serve the nations as a special ops church that produces
and sends special ops Christians to the nations imbued
with the highest ideals of Christian love and friendship.
We teach teamwork to special ops Christians through
a fully integrated curriculum of academic and practical
studies that is designed to release people with their individual responsibilities to work within the structure of team
ministry.

We challenge people to achieve their full potential in
spirit, soul, and body. We provide a comprehensive support
system to ensure individual growth and success.

We value the cultural and ethnic diversity of the people
and nations we serve. We are dedicated to winning their
hearts and minds with love. We, the people of the special
ops church team, recognize Jesus Christ as the chief
Cornerstone of our reputation for excellence. We take pride
in sending the highest quality of special ops Christians to
disciple the nations.[4]

Note how the vision of the special ops church lines up with the
grand strategic objective of Jesus Christ. The vision clearly states that
special ops Christians are highly motivated to disciple the nations for
Jesus Christ. It is these dedicated disciples who make up the special
ops church and usher in the kingdom of God's rule upon the earth.

The objective should always be the driving principle of war. It must
be the thing the special ops church, corporately, and the special ops
Christian, individually, aim for in spiritual warfare. The objective
must be clearly defined, decisive, and attainable. The ultimate military
objective in natural warfare is the destruction of the enemy's armed
forces and his will to fight. The same is expected in spiritual warfare.

The objectives of each small operation must contribute to the
grand strategic objective. These intermediate objectives must be

attainable and contribute to the grand strategic objective in a direct, quick, and economical way. Through worship, intercessory prayer, and fasting, our spiritual enemy is removed. Apostolically planting or setting churches in order are intermediate objectives made up of small operations that have an impact on the success of the grand strategic objective. Selection of an intermediate objective by a special ops church is based upon consideration of the means available, the enemy, and the area of operations.

The objective needs attainable goals in a good plan of action. Every apostolic leader must understand and clearly define his objective and consider each contemplated action in light of that objective. The loss of focus on the objective is very damaging.

The nine principles of war (including the objective) have two applications. It is imperative that we relate each of the nine principles of war to the objective. This is best accomplished by simply asking the following question: does my action in utilizing any of the nine principles of war sufficiently advance the grand strategic objective of Jesus Christ, that being the discipling of the nations?

1. Strategy

Leadership first agrees upon the mission, vision, and guiding principles; and this forms the foundation for the strategic plan. Then the special ops church develops goals, strategies, and objectives that will enable the church to bridge the gap between the present and the future special ops church, as described in its vision.

By definition, strategy is the preparation for war and the direction of war. This is where the second part of the definition of the objective must be carefully addressed. Strategic planning addresses attainable goals in a good plan of action. It focuses leaders on the methods to achieve an ideal vision (what the special ops church should be and could be) ten and twenty years into the future. Long-range planning for a special ops church may only mean one year in the future or the next budget submission.

2. Tactics

This is the application of action taken in specific battles and operations. Every Marine Corps officer is taught a simple five-paragraph order for tactical operations. I used this successfully in Vietnam to brief my men prior to each mission. The acronym for the five-paragraph order is SMEACC, which stands for:

- Situation: Briefly define what is going on in the tactical area of operation you will be working in.
- Mission: State what the specific secondary objective is to fulfilling the grand strategic objective. The mission is usually made up of one or more secondary objectives.
- Execution: List each intermediate step in pursuit of a successful mission.
- Administration: Develop schedules and reservations for lodging, transportation, food, dates, and times pertinent to the operation.
- Command: Announce the chain of command or authority structure for the mission.
- Communications: State how the team will communicate with one another and those who are supporting the operation from afar (e.g., through cell phones, e-mail, or the like).[5]

Although SMEACC may seem simplistic, it is highly effective in organizing a special ops team for any operation. Remember, you are in a spiritual war and the way you carry out your tactical objective concerning specific battles and operations is very important to your victory at the strategic or big-picture level.

The following is the actual SMEACC my wife and I used when preparing for a visit to an established "battle front" in South Africa in December 2007. The team members and our special ops church leadership and intercessors receive copies of the SMEACC. (Our special ops church receives a separate SMEACC spelling out the plan to operate the church while its lead apostle is on the battlefield.)

Situation

Over the past seven years, we have established trusted relationships with four apostolic leaders in Gauteng Province, South Africa. My wife and I, along with the support of our U.S. apostolic coalition of churches, have formed an African coalition with these leaders. Apostle Rob Enos of Greater Works Christian Church in Lancaster, California, has been a major supporter and builder of both our U.S. and African coalitions. Through a humanitarian organization the International Children's Aid Network, Inc., we are currently partnering with this South African coalition to build the first of many Children's Villages in South Africa, which will be the home to hundreds of orphans. Now is the time to visit our South African coalition and review our progress on construction of the first Children's Village in the black township of Soweto.

Mission

The mission of this trip is to review our progress in sheltering, feeding, clothing, and providing educational and medical assistance to orphans who will live at our Children's Village in Soweto.

Execution

- Contact the South African coalition and inform them of the visit.
- Procure airline reservations.
- Select the team that will be going on the South African mission and inform the prayer intercessors.
- Hold training sessions for team members.
- Gather funds to pay for transportation, lodging, and food for the mission.
- Contact the South African coalition with the dates and time of arrival and departure and have them make reservations for lodging in Johannesburg.
- Make sure immunization and passport records are up to date.

- Arrange for transportation to the airport when leaving the U.S. and pick-up transportation upon our return.

Administration

- Make sure the team is prepared with plane tickets, updated immunization records, and passports.
- Arrange airport pickup for arrival and departure with the South African coalition.
- Arrange lodging and food through the South African coalition.
- Submit a suggested itinerary to the South African coalition for their input.

Command

- Make very clear who is first in command of the mission.
- Make clear who is second and third in command and state when they would be expected to pick up the leadership role.

Communications

Be very clear who is designated to make reports to the church back in the U.S. Designate who should take computers and international cell phones and explain how they are used. Since we all have different perceptions of how the mission is going and different standards concerning what should be shared publicly and what should be on a need-to-know basis, only the team leader will make situation reports to the home front.

THE CHOICE OF THE RIGHT PERSONNEL TO ACCOMPLISH THE MISSION IS VERY IMPORTANT

Late in the summer of 1969 in Vietnam, my recon team was not only very experienced but also very successful. We had captured the most prisoners, [and] had the largest number of enemy sighting and confirmed kills. After fending off weeks of appeals from an inexperienced radioman who worked in our command and communications bunker I finally agreed to take him on a patrol.

The second day into the mission we made point contact with the enemy, killing one of them. For the next eight hours a much larger enemy unit pursued us. They were always about fifty yards behind us during the chase. They randomly fired their weapons hoping to hit us in the process. Finally at dusk after hours of escape-and-evade tactics, trying to lose the much larger enemy unit, disaster nearly struck. After climbing our way through the thick jungle terrain, we only had to get up one more hill to escape. I was leading the team up the steep hill when I looked behind me. The inexperienced radioman had stopped moving up the hill. He had let the exhaustion of the chase strip him of his dignity. Now his actions had the whole team strung out in open sight on the hillside. I crawled back to the radioman and grabbed the radio off his back. Then I commanded him to move out. I pulled him up the hill and got the rest of the team moving behind us. Whose fault was this almost fatal situation? It was my fault. I never should have taken him on the patrol.[6]

Special ops Christianity can be just as dangerous as a recon patrol in Vietnam. We must be very discerning about whom we take on what mission. They must be ready to go. Every special ops team member must be a disciple who knows the Word. They must know what is appropriate spiritually. It is too late once a team member is ten thousand miles from home to teach them the principles that are being covered in this book. It is too late for the special ops church to reel in someone who is already on a mission but not really prepared for the intensity of battle. The apostle Paul had a problem keeping John Mark on the team at one time during his missionary journeys.

Now Paul and his companions sailed from Paphos and came to Pergo Pamphylia. And John [Mark] separated himself from them and went back to Jerusalem.

—ACTS 13:13, AMP

How do special ops Christians arrive at a personal objective for their lives that prepares them for service in special ops missions?

Wherein ye greatly rejoice, though now for a season, if need be, ye are in heaviness through temptations: That the trial of your faith, being much more precious than of gold that perisheth, though it be tried with fire, might be found unto praise and honor and glory at the appearing of Jesus Christ: Whom having not seen, ye love; in whom, though now ye see him not, yet believing, ye rejoice with joy unspeakable and full of glory: Receiving the end of your faith, even the salvation of your souls.

—1 PETER 1:6–9

The objective of a special ops Christian has everything to do with 1 Peter 1:9: "Receiving the end of your faith."

God wants to see us begin in faith and end in faith, which is why the special ops Christian's personal objective is "receiving the end of his faith," or the manifestation of whatever he has taken aim at in his personal battle. The special ops Christian's faith, in moving toward the manifestation of the objective, will be tested by the devil, our enemy, who would rather have us operate in fear. While God wants special ops Christians to operate in faith and produce anything of positive value in our lives, the devil must have the special ops Christian operate in fear to produce anything of negative value in our lives. The biggest fear that Satan may throw at the special ops Christian is fear that the Word of God will not produce what it promises, which is the "receiving the end of their faith."

The Bible gives the Special Ops Christian some great encouragement concerning the testing by fire of our faith while on our journey to the manifestation of our objective.

There hath no temptation taken you but such as is common to man: but God is faithful, who will not suffer you to be tempted above that ye are able; but will with temptation also make a way to escape, that ye may be able to bear it.

—1 CORINTHIANS 10:13

First Corinthians 10:13 tells the special ops Christian that God would not allow him to take the test unless He knew he could pass the test. It tells us we are able to bear the temptation.

As a special ops Christian, we must realize the test is being applied to our flesh, not our spirit. God has condemned Satan and his operation to remain in the boundaries of the natural realm, that arena that is natural or common to man. The special ops Christian is not bound in the natural realm but has full authority as a believer in the supernatural realm. Jesus disarmed Satan from having full use of the power he once had to tempt, test, and put pressure on the people of God. He can only use what is common to man, what is in the natural realm. The enemy is a sitting duck, and when God's people get a fix on his position they can rain down worship, intercessory prayer, proclamations, and decrees of judgment on his head. The special ops Christian has the authority to cast the enemy out of his ministry, family, business, and his or her life in general.

According to Isaiah 10:27, the special ops Christian has burden lifting and yoke destroying anointing, as well as the promise that he will receive at the end of His faith, which is the manifestation of the objective.[7]

THE HOW, WHEN, WHERE, AND WHY OF SPECIAL OPS CHRISTIANITY

How and where does the special ops Christian form his objective?

The objective is formed by the planting of the promised Word into the special ops Christian's heart through his or her eyes, ears, and mouth. (See Proverbs 4:20–24.)

Proverbs 4:23 warns us, "Keep thy heart with all diligence; for out of it are the issues of life." The special ops Christian's objective is one of these issues of life whose accuracy and success are dependent upon a pure heart seeded with the incorruptible seed of the Word of God. Allowing only positive words to be formed in your heart and allowing only positive words to come out of your mouth is a very important issue of life. Luke 17:21 says, "The kingdom of God is within you." The Amplified Bible states the same verse this way: "For behold, the Kingdom of God is within you [in your hearts]." The special ops Christian plants the Word into the soil of his heart. If physical healing is the objective, then he plants healing scriptures into his heart. If a special mission to the nations is the objective, then he plants scriptures about finances into his heart. If a better marriage is the objective, then he plants scriptures on marriage into his heart. In due season, it will break through the door of the heart into the physical world and he will see the manifestation of his objective.

Why does the special ops Christian guard his mouth?

For good or for evil, these forces create the life we live. Out of the heart the mouth speaks the issues (or forces) of life (Prov. 4:23). The heart or spirit of a man is the key area of his or her being.

How does the special ops Christian guard his heart?

Proverbs 4:23 makes it clear that we are to guard our hearts "with all diligence." Diligence is a steady, constant effort to guard your heart. It concerns your vertical relationship with God. When your vertical relationship is right, then your horizontal relationships (with brothers and sisters) will be much more successful.

How should a special ops Christian guard his mouth in reference to the heart?

When you speak, you are writing either for good or for evil on your heart.

My tongue is the pen of a ready writer.

—PSALM 45:1

Death and life are in the power of the tongue.

—PROVERBS 18:21

Put away from thee a forward mouth, and perverse lips put far from thee.

—PROVERBS 4:24

How does a special ops Christian form his objectives so they are effective in the kingdom of God?

And thou, Solomon my son, know thou the God of thy father, and serve him with a perfect heart and with a willing mind: for the LORD searcheth all hearts, and understandeth all the imaginations of the thoughts: if thou seek him, he will be found of thee; but if thou forsake him, he will cast thee off for ever.

—1 CHRONICLES 28:9

This verse tells us that the heart of man is connected to his imaginations, and his imaginations are connected to his thoughts. The key words are *hearts*, *imaginations*, and *thoughts*.

God is checking our hearts. He understands all the imaginations of our thoughts. The *imaginations of our thoughts* merely refers to the creativity of our imaginations through our thought processes.

How does a special ops Christian prepare his heart for effective thoughts?

O LORD of Abraham, Isaac, and of Israel, our fathers, keep this for ever in the imagination of the thoughts of the heart of thy people, and prepare their heart unto thee.

—1 CHRONICLES 29:18

There is a progression: words enter into a man's heart through his eyes, ears, and mouth, then they form and effect thoughts. When you speak God's words, you cast down the devil's words. Words produce thoughts and thoughts come together and construct images.

As he thinketh in his heart, so is he.

—PROVERBS 23:7

How does a special ops Christian prepare his heart for effective images?

Bondages, or strongholds, are nothing but houses constructed of thoughts.

> For though we walk in the flesh, we do not war after the flesh: (For the weapons of our warfare are not carnal, but mighty through God to the pulling down of strong holds;) Casting down imaginations, and every high thing that exalteth itself against the knowledge of God, and bringing into captivity every thought to the obedience of Christ.
>
> —2 CORINTHIANS 10:3–5

The incorruptible seeds of the Word of God are the weapons of our warfare. If you stay with the Word of God long enough, your thoughts will produce an image in the realm of the imagination, which will become manifest.

Should the special ops Christian use his imagination, or is it dangerous?

The root word for *imagination* is "image." It may be seen throughout the Bible that God always deals with images or thoughts that produce images. Proverbs 2:10 says, "For skillful and godly Wisdom shall enter into your heart, and knowledge shall be pleasant to you" (AMP). This kind of wisdom enters into the heart by the way of thought-provoking images. Proverbs 6:15–19 warns us, saying, "Therefore shall his calamity come suddenly; suddenly shall he be broken without remedy. These six things doth the LORD hate: yea, seven are an abomination unto him: A proud look, a lying tongue, and hands that shed innocent blood, An heart that deviseth wicked imaginations, feet that be swift in running to mischief, A false witness that speaketh lies, and he that soweth discord among bretheren." Meditating on the Word of God, or rolling God's Word over and over in our mind, will create godly images.

You can get an inner image of your covenant out of Deuteronomy 28. Most of the church world has not meditated on God's Word, which is why they are missing out on the manifestation of God's promises.

> This book of the law shall not depart out of thy mouth; but thou shalt meditate therein day and night, that thou mayest observe to do according to all that is written therein: for then thou shalt make thy way prosperous, and then thou shalt have good success.
>
> —Joshua 1:8

The attention God gives to the power of man's imagination can be found in Genesis 11:3–6:

> And they said one to another, Go to, let us make brick, and burn them thoroughly. And they had brick for stone, and slime had they for mortar. And they said, Go to, let us build us a city and a tower, whose top may reach unto heaven; and let us make us a name, lest we be scattered abroad upon the face of the whole earth. And the LORD came down to see the city and the tower, which the children of men builded. And the LORD said, Behold, the people is one, and they have all one language; and this they begin to do: and now nothing will be restrained from them, which they have imagined to do.

How does the special ops Christian nurture images sent from God?

Images are stored in the imagination in blueprint form. In Genesis 11:6, we read that God saw the blueprint for the city and tower in the imaginations of the men even though it had not yet manifested, and God was very unhappy with that image.

Remember, your image is the blueprint of your objective, and it is your hope.

Faith is the substance of things hoped for, the evidence of things not seen.

—HEBREWS 11:1

You need the hope, the blueprint or image, to place your faith in. You also need the Word of God, which is confirmation that your hope is born out of the incorruptible seed that always yields a harvest. Whatever you imagine to do can be brought out of the unseen realm of your heart and manifest in the seen, or natural, realm. Once the special ops Christian has the image, manifestation is right around the corner. The image is always the prerequisite of manifestation.

How does Satan steal images and objectives from our hearts?

Most men don't have an objective for their lives because they won't read God's Word long enough to get an image.

There are five things Satan uses to destroy the image in our hearts. They are found in Mark 4:14–19. Guard your heart against them.

- affliction
- persecutions
- cares of this world
- deceitfulness of riches
- lust of riches

The information we have just covered is extremely important for developing a special ops capability in any local church, either large or small. A special ops team is only as good as the weakest link in the chain, or more specifically, the weakest team member. There is much work left to accomplish in the earth concerning the kingdom of God. The Lord will entrust much to churches and Christians who are disciplined and trained to handle spiritual conflict.

CHAPTER 6

THE THREE-PHASE OFFENSIVE

LAOTIAN BORDER, FORTY-FOUR MILES SOUTHWEST OF DA NANG, SOUTH VIETNAM, JUNE 17–19, 1969

On June 17, 1969, four First Force Recon teams were inserted by helicopter deep into enemy-controlled territory along the Laotian Border. This was the deepest penetration that any Marine reconnaissance unit made since the war had officially begun in 1965. My six-man team was one of the Force Recon units that were dropped into the middle of the hostile area forty-four miles South West of Da Nang. The teams' missions ranged from locating an enemy tank and fuel park to finding a prisoner of war camp where U.S. pilots were imprisoned. My mission was the suspected POW camp located about two thousand meters from my insert landing zone. An army Huey helicopter was rigged with sixty-foot cable ladders rolled up on its left and right sides and attached to the skids of the craft, which were our stairway into the mountainous jungle. We walked down the ladders trapeze-style. My point man and my secondary radioman went down first. Then the primary radioman and I started down. At about thirty feet above the ground, my radioman fell off the ladder and piled into my point man beneath him. The helicopter started to crash because of the sudden shift in weight. I clung to the ladder until the pilot steadied the craft. When I reached the ground, I had two men wounded with head and back injuries. The radioman needed MedEvac assistance, while the point man looked good enough to continue the mission. I learned as we began to move out on the patrol that the point man was wounded worse than he had let on. The MedEvac helicopter drew a lot of attention as it hovered above the team at treetop level and hoisted the wounded radioman to safety in a basket. Everything about the mission had changed in an instant. We had lost the element of surprise, and a major breach in security occurred when the MedEvac helicopter did its thing. My team was now forced into an offensive mode much sooner than expected. In the next forty-eight hours of the patrol, I would use all three phases of the principle of war known as the offensive.[1]

OFFENSIVE

The act of aggressively seizing, retaining, and exploiting momentum and initiative in battle[2]

The three phases of the principle of war known as the offensive are:

- mass-power,
- economy of force, and
- maneuver.[3]

Maneuver

The mobility and flexibility of force, in an effort to achieve objectives[4]

Maneuver was the first phase of the offensive I employed after my radioman went to MedEvac. I completely changed the route to the top of the mountain. I knew the enemy was probably setting up defenses on the ridgeline looming above us. I chose a route that took us deep into a ravine that would have been impossible for the enemy to follow us into undetected. This was a classic use of maneuver.

Economy of force

> Effective use of force that overwhelms the opposition while preserving resources[5]

Rather than putting all the team's energy into racing up and over the ridgeline, I moved the team very slowly. My platoon sergeant, Eugene Ayers, carefully covered up the jungle vegetation we had to tunnel through on our hands and knees. Late in the day we surfaced on a narrow jungle shelf with steep ravines on both sides. The way was clear to move the team up to the top of the ridge, but we were losing light and my point man was showing signs of a serious head wound. I stopped the team and we spent the night on that narrow but defendable piece of ground. By the next morning, two of the four teams that had been inserted the day before were in heavy contact with the enemy. Phantom jets flew over our position for several hours dumping tons of ordnance around the beleaguered teams. One team had found an enemy tank park. The other team met an enemy platoon and lost their point man, Lance Corporal Dennis Murphy, to enemy fire. Murphy had covered for the team's escape. Every one of his team members had been shot, and Dennis Murphy, age nineteen, had placed himself between his friends and advancing enemy soldiers. The team leader had taken three AK-47 rounds in the stomach but managed to keep the team moving to an emergency extraction helicopter-landing zone.

All of this activity so deep inside enemy-controlled territory spelled disaster for all our missions. The enemy knew we had invaded their base camp area and they didn't want any of us to get out of there alive. Our company commander warned us to stay where we were until the other teams had been safely extracted. Knowing my team would have to use mass-power I began to study the map in preparation to run strategic air strikes around our position.[6]

Mass-Power

The release of force in the most effective time, place and manner, to overwhelm the opposition[7]

Sure enough, within hours the enemy began probing our position. I called for immediate air support and got it. Refueled Phantom jets were suddenly flying over my position dropping one thousand-pound bombs above, below, and on both sides of my position, making it virtually impossible for the enemy to break through. Suddenly a CH-46 helicopter with a 140-foot cable latter hanging under it was hovering above us. The ladder dangled thirty feet above our heads, and quickly the enemy above us turned all his firepower on the vulnerable helicopter, almost bringing the big bird down. The chopper's crew chief was badly wounded as the helicopter powered its way out of the kill zone. Once again I directed the Phantom jets as they saturation-bombed the ridge above us. I was massing all the power available to me as I directed the air strikes on the enemy's positions above me. Once again a CH-46 helicopter appeared. This time a 180-foot cargo strap called a SPIE Rig dangled beneath the big bird. The strap, with its D-rings attached, reached us. We quickly hooked up to the D-rings with ropes and snap links, and the helicopter pulled us straight up and out of the jungle like puppets. This was the moment in battle that the Principle of War known as mass-power was being used to its fullest extent. Mass-power included the Phantom jets, gun birds and COBRA helicopters, plus tons of bombs to open up the opportunity for my team to clear the jungle canopy dangling from the SPIE Rig like circus performers. Within minutes we were flying above the mountains at better than three thousand feet.[8]

It is very important for special ops Christians and special ops churches to know how to use the offensive and its three phases in battle. "I'm just waiting on God" is an overused cliché very familiar to most Christians. Without the principle of war known as the offensive, waiting can become a dangerous game. The special ops church must understand the pitfalls of waiting. The enemy must not deceive special ops Christians into a posture of non-activity. Waiting is usually a defensive posture where the act of aggressively seizing, retaining, and exploiting momentum and the initiative in battle can be lost. A corporate vulnerability is opened up when a church loses momentum. The individual Christian's situation can be further compromised when he or she loses momentum. This lack of momentum can eventually begin to drain a church and its members of the power they need for their own ministries, businesses, and marriages. When this begins to happen, it is time to reconnect with the mission and vision of the special ops church.

Remember, a defensive posture is only supposed to be temporary for purposes of rest and regrouping for further offensive action. Offensive action is necessary to achieve decisive results and to maintain freedom of action. Freedom of action means that the church has the freedom to choose from a number of offensive options. This keeps the enemy guessing what the next move will be and is the key to the special ops church's victory. Freedom of action allows leadership in the church to go on the offensive by exercising initiative and imposing the Lord's will on the enemy. The church can set the pace and determine the course of the battle. The offensive allows the commander to exploit the enemy's weakness by rapidly changing a situation to meet unexpected developments.

The key to understanding the principle of the offensive is actually contained in the first sentence of one of its supporting facts: "offensive action is needed to achieve decisive results and to maintain freedom of action."[9] The task of achieving decisive results requires a basic appreciation for the difference between the postures of the strategic offensive and the tactical offensive. The offensive is strategic when it leads directly to the political objective or the purpose for which the war is being waged. When the offensive is tactical, each battlefield victory does not necessarily lead directly to peace but is considered a means that eventually leads to peace. The offensive action that does not lead directly to the objective must be considered tactical, not strategic. The tactical is necessary and often leads to the larger scale of strategic planning that does lead directly to peace and victory. We can summarize this by saying that no matter how insignificant a tactical move might seem, it may help win the battle.

Understanding the strategic and tactical offensive and defensive is worth knowing and understanding.

In Baron von der Goltz's *The Conduct of War*, he comes up with some revealing formulas concerning the strategic/tactical offensive and defensive. (We are not interested in his politics, only the theory he developed.) Once again, let's use Matthew 28 and the discipling of the nations as our overall strategic objective as we review the success of strategic/tactical objectives from the offensive and defensive postures. Please take a moment and try to understand these principles.

- When we are in the strategic-defensive and tactical-defensive postures, there will be the complete absence of victory.
- When we are in the posture of strategic-defensive and tactical-offensive, there will be victory on the battlefield without general results for the campaign or strategic objective.
- When we are in a posture of strategic-offensive and tactical-defensive, the general situation is favorable for a victory, which, however, is without results because the fighting power of the enemy is not impaired.
- Strategic-offensive and tactical-offensive (as a posture) result in the destruction of the enemy and conquest of his territory. Maintaining the offensive initiative is very key to disciplining the nations.[10]

Understanding the Times and Seasons

In further reference to discipling nations, let's look at the following scripture:

> Then cometh the end, when he shall have delivered up the kingdom to God, even the Father; when he shall have put down all rule and all authority and power. For he must reign, till he hath put all enemies under His feet. The last enemy that shall be destroyed is death.
>
> —1 Corinthians 15:24–26

We are somewhat in a military cleanup mode here on Earth. We use supernatural weapons to fight spiritual battles, until ultimately all of His enemies will be made a footstool for His feet. Remember, a good offensive strategy allows us to set the pace and determine the course of action. The last enemy that shall be destroyed is death, which we will preach to destruction.

Let's review the victory over death that will provide the political objectives of the kingdom of God. First Corinthians 15:44 explains that our natural body is sown like a seed and is raised a spiritual body, and death will have no longer have power over Christians. The image of the first Adam will pale in contrast to the glory the Second Adam, Jesus Christ, who will manifest through us. To this we say with Paul, "O, death, where is thy sting? O grave, where is thy victory?" (1 Cor. 15:55).

How will we know when our offensive action has accomplished the grand strategic objective of Jesus Christ? We will see the Great Commission fulfilled and the kingdom of God manifesting itself in all glory, power, rule, and authority. You will know because God's way of doing things will visually overtake the corrupt world system as righteous men and women begin to run the institutions that control the nations. You will begin to see the mission of the special ops church fulfilled as people from every nation are developed morally and physically while being imbued with an unconditional love for mankind, found in the triune God. Special ops Christians will recognize the success of their mission when they see their code of conduct operating in areas of accountability, loyalty, integrity, and teamwork. This will help empower Christian people to assume the highest responsibilities in the kingdom of God, especially in areas of command, citizenship, and government throughout the nations.

Presumptuous theories of eschatology or beliefs about the End Times can have a devastating effect on Jesus' overall strategic objective. Premature exit strategies from the battlefield of planet Earth can change all strategic and tactical postures. The special ops church must occupy by taking the gospel to the nations. Remember that we must be on the offensive while we occupy this territory.

The two most dangerous moments for my Force Recon team during combat missions in Vietnam came at the beginning of the patrol during the team's insert into enemy-controlled territory and on the extract of the team while exiting enemy-controlled territory via helicopter. When my men thought they were leaving the battlefield, they had a tendency to relax. Often, the enemy would wait for that moment of letdown to attack us. The best policy is not to always be thinking about Jesus coming to take His church away. A special ops Christian must be confident that Jesus will deliver him out of harm's way while he fights the good fight of faith on the battlefield. The offensive action of that fight should be directed toward the grand strategic objective of discipling the nations and the establishment of the kingdom of God in the earth.

Once again, there are three methods to employ the offensive. They are mass-power, economy of force, and maneuver. They are best understood in concert. When viewed separately, they are often misinterpreted. Read carefully the following expanded definitions.

- Mass-power is the release of force in the most effective time, place, and manner to overwhelm the opposition. It is the release of superior prayer and worship power at a critical time and place for a decisive purpose. Then the special ops church is ready to release its special ops team onto the battlefield with the gospel anywhere in the world.

- Economy of force refers to the effective use of force that overwhelms the opposition while preserving resources. With proper application of all the principles of war, economy of force can give the numerically inferior special ops church decisive spiritual superiority. It isn't always wise to throw every resource into one battle. Manpower, finances, and prayer should be measured out in a way that allows the special ops church to answer a counterattack of the enemy.

- Maneuver is mobility and flexibility of force in an effort to achieve the objective. It exploits successes, preserves freedom of action, and reduces vulnerability. Maneuver disposes force in such a manner that it places the enemy at a relative disadvantage. It can save manpower and material. It requires flexibility in organization, administrative support, command, and control. It is the antithesis of permanence of location and implies avoidance of stereotyped patterns of operation.[11]

A SCRIPTURAL LOOK AT A TYPICAL SPECIAL OPS CHRISTIAN

Ultimately it will be special ops Christians moving in the offensive under the guidance of the Holy Spirit and the special ops church that will be taking the battle to the enemy. Special ops Christians come in all shapes and sizes. The following Scripture is an excellent description of such a Christian.

> For ye see your calling brethren, how that not many wise men after the flesh, not many mighty, not many noble, are called: But God hath chosen the foolish things of the world to confound the wise; and God hath chosen the weak things of the world to confound the things which are mighty; And

base things of the world, and things which are despised, hath God chosen, yea, and things which are not, to bring to nought things that are: That no flesh should glory in His presence.

—1 Corinthians 1:26–29

Note that the language of this scripture has the chosen special ops Christian moving in the offensive to:

1. confound the wise,
2. bring to naught things that are, and
3. confound things that are mighty.

Properly releasing the offensive in the spirit realm is a major key to success in spiritual warfare. Jesus said, "I will give you the keys of the kingdom of heaven; and whatever you bind (declare to be improper and unlawful) on earth must be what is already bound in heaven; and whatever you loose (declare lawful) on earth must be what is already loosed in heaven" (Matt. 16:19, AMP).

God's perspective of things is different than the world's perspective of things. God chooses Christians and churches to decree and declare according to the Word the things that are not, to bring to naught the things that are. This method is evident throughout the entire Bible. God uses things that have not been manifested (things you cannot see with your natural eyes). Through the mouth of a special ops church or Christian, God is using those things you cannot comprehend with your sensory mechanisms to create new situations and circumstances. God is using things that are naught—which means "zero" or "nothing"—to create new things. At the same time, He is using things not yet manifested to bring to nothing the things that are manifested. By the mass-power of God's Word, which you cannot see, the special ops Christian can reduce to nothing the visible manifestations of his enemy the devil's work in the Earth realm. As long as the special ops Christian can see it, he can decree or declare the spoken Word to change it. He can apply mass-power on the offensive to exercise initiative and impose Christ's will on His enemy.

If the special ops Christian can see it, he can change it. People may be able to see the poverty in their life, but God has a method to change what they see. Others may see inadequate employment in their life, but the special ops Christian can deal with that by praying and speaking the Word. The special ops Christian can shake nations by decreeing the Word of God.

> You shall…decree a thing, and it shall be established.
> —JOB 22:28, AMP

No matter what religious system, level of poverty, or oppression a nation is under, if the special ops church can see the problem, they can change it. There is no situation over any nation in which there isn't a way out through the mass-power offensive action of God's Word. The special ops church that prays and speaks the Word of God over nations will see positive changes take place.

> We having the same spirit of faith, according as it is written,
> I believed, and therefore have I spoken; we also believe, and
> therefore speak.
> —2 CORINTHIANS 4:13–14

If the special ops Christian believes what has entered his heart through his eyes, ears, and mouth concerning the Word of God, then he must speak it out to effect change.

An example of God using this mass-power of His Word to create things can be found in Romans 4:17.

> As it is written, I have made you [Abraham] the father of
> many nations. [He was appointed our father] in the sight of
> God in Whom he believed, Who gives life to the dead and
> speaks of the nonexistent things that [He has foretold and
> promised] as if they [already] existed. (AMP)

God called Abraham the father of many nations and broke his fatherless state with the mass-power of His Word.

The special ops Christian looks at something that is not seen through the Word of God. You may not be able to see the healing, successful business, ministry, or marriage but can comprehend, through the Word, what you cannot comprehend through the natural.

- Concerning healing, the Word says by the stripes of Jesus Christ you were healed. (See 1 Peter 2:24.)
- Concerning discipling of nations, the Word says, "Every knee should bow...and every tongue confess that Jesus Christ is Lord" (Phil. 2:10–11, NIV).
- Concerning debt, the Word says, "You will lend to many nations but will borrow from none" (Deut. 28:12).

The temporal situations and circumstances of this life are just that—they are temporal, or temporary. Sickness and death are only temporary, and the special ops Christian can speak the Word over it, bringing it to naught.

Religious persecution against Christians in China, Cuba, Iran, Iraq, or India is only temporary according to Matthew 28:19, where Jesus says, "All power is given unto me in heaven and in earth."

We need to recognize that the world's situation is only temporary. According to the Word of God, it will change.

Jesus said that the least in the kingdom of God was greater than John the Baptist. The special ops church and Christian has all the power that he needs to accomplish his mission by going on the offensive through praying and speaking the Word. The tools of the enemy, such as poverty, sickness, false religions, and threatening armies of terrorists, are all temporary in the light of God's Word. We cannot allow the devil to thwart our offensive strategy and tactics by convincing us that God's Word doesn't work. The mass-power of God's Word brings to naught those problems, which are seen.

Romans 4:17 states, "Even God, who quickeneth the dead, and calleth those things which be not as though they were." This scripture says that God creates by calling "those things which be not as though they were." It says that God called. If God called, then the special ops Christian and church must also go on the offensive and call forth the Word concerning what we want to see happen. God uses this method of calling. He began calling Abraham the father of many nations before he even had a child. Genesis 1:3 records that "God said, 'Let there be light: and there was light.'" In both of these instances God called that which was not as though it was—and there came nations out of Abraham and light out of darkness. Calling out those things that are, such as barrenness and darkness, and declaring God's Word over them is an offensive tactic. Getting an entire church doing it is mass-power.

> But the righteousness which is of faith speaketh on this wise. Say not in thine heart, Who shall ascend into heaven? (that is, to bring Christ down from above:) Or, Who shall descend into the deep? (that is, to bring up Christ again from the dead.) But what saith it? The word is nigh thee, even in thy mouth, and in thy heart: That is, the word of faith, which we preach; That if thou shalt confess with thy mouth the Lord Jesus, and shalt believe in thine heart that God hath raised him from the dead, thou shalt be saved.
>
> —ROMANS 10:6–10

The special ops Christian and church must not sit idly by thinking that Jesus is going to come down from heaven to accomplish what He has empowered His church and His people to accomplish on the earth. The death, burial, and resurrection were Jesus' job here on Earth. Discipling nations is the church's job. Jesus is the Head of the church and is seated at the right hand of the Father in heaven. We are His body, the church, and as the body we have shoulders. According Isaiah 9:6, the government is upon His shoulders. The special ops church is the body of Christ in the earth and has the governmental authority to accomplish the work of the Head, Jesus, here on Earth.

Dr. Bill and Barbara Peters became a team on May 15, 1971.

Bill Peters learned about teamwork on the gridiron in the 1960's. He is pictued here with lifelong friend and teammate Leland Wallace. Peters and Wallace played on the same teams in high school and college, joined the Marine Corps together, and attended Officer Candidate School at Quantico, VA in 1967. Wallace became a Marine Corps fighter pilot and was killed in 1969.

Lt. Peters, center photo, pictured with his prisoner acquisition team August, 1969. The team successfully captured a high ranking enemy soldier the following day after a fierce fire fight with a company sized enemy force.

Lt. Bill Peters leads his team high in the mountains of the Thong Duc corridor, a major entry point for enemy troops crossing the Vietnam and Laotian border in December, 1969.

Bill Peters speaks about team work before First Force Recon Company marines at Camp Pendleton Oceanside, CA, in 2001.

Bill Peters' team in May, 1969, calls for air and artillery strikes on a large enemy force moving in a valley below a permanent recon observation post high in the Que Son Mountains of South Vietnam.

Lt. Bill Peters' recon team disarmed an enemy soldier of this Russian made AK-47 assault rifle that nearly took Peters' life on a mission deep in enemy controlled territory August 10, 1969.

Lt. Peters gave his life to Jesus Christ just 18 months after this photo was taken in September, 1969, at the First Force Recon Company, special ops compound near Da Nang, South Vietnam.

CHAPTER 7

SECURITY, SURPRISE, SIMPLICITY

APRIL 20, 1969, AN HOA, SOUTH VIETNAM

Tension was palatable in the First Force Recon Company staff and officers meeting. The question that hung in the air like a big balloon was why the N.V.A. seemed to be waiting in every conceivable landing zone in First Force's tactical area of responsibility. Finally, Lt. Ric Miller, a veteran of the war, broke the silence with this revelation. He asked, "Why is the Chief of Duc Duc province on the cc list of all the operations orders that are being given to the recon teams?" Miller went on to say, "You know our operation orders have the grid coordinates of all our helicopter insert zones, and further, the chief of Duc Duc has always been a sympathizer of the enemy Viet Cong. Bingo! A huge violation had been uncovered concerning the principle of war known as security. When the chief was suddenly removed from the cc of the company operation orders, the enemy no longer was controlling all the landing zones. The principle of war known as surprise was also returned to the recon teams. The principle of war known as simplicity was also at work here. A simple deletion of the name of the chief from the operation order solved a major tactical and even lethal problem.[1]

Security: the protection of everything vital to the accomplishment of your objectives

Surprise: the launch of an offensive against the opposition in place and manner that they are unprepared for, at an unexpected time

Simplicity: the organization of plans as well as communications of orders in a simple, clear, and concise manner

The principle of war known as surprise is extremely important in war. The principles of security and surprise are reciprocal, meaning they work together. Many military strategists link them together and even identify security as an element of surprise. In addition to the other rules of conduct, surprise has both tactical and strategic application.

Although surprise, as a key element of success in war, is highly attractive in theory, in reality, it is difficult to achieve. Surprise must be considered basically as a tactical device. It is interesting to note that strategic surprise is a rarity in conventional warfare these days. Modern technology and surveillance (i.e., satellites and radar), plus the time it takes to mount an offensive and trying to mass troops secretly, makes surprise very difficult for conventional warfare. In this instance, the science of war can trump the art of war.

Nonconventional special ops warfare allows us to employ the principle of surprise. This kind of warfare, also known as asymmetrical warfare, tries to surprise the opposition and then impose their will upon them. Ideally, surprise should strike the enemy's center of gravity. The center of gravity is the area of strength an opponent is resting upon. Some organizations' line of communication is their center of gravity, while supply lines may be the center of gravity for another organization. Offensive action generated by surprise can destabilize the enemy's center of gravity.[2]

Surprise can mean a tactical defeat for the special ops Christian while at the same time signaling a strategic victory for the special ops church. For example, the death of Jesus on the cross seemed like a horrible tactical defeat, but it was in fact a powerful strategic victory for the Father and His Son. Even though for a while Jesus' enemies enjoyed a tactical victory after His death on the cross, the resurrection of Jesus was a great strategic victory. The redemption of mankind was a second great strategic victory. John 15:13 explains this tactical sacrifice, saying, "Greater love hath no man than this, that a man lay down his life for his friends."

Surprise can dramatically shift the balance of combat power. The special ops church must have its tactical objective ready to manifest. This means apostolic vision must be clear concerning the spiritual operation the church is engaged in. When employing the principle of surprise, special ops Christians can strike the enemy at a time, place, and in a manner for which he is not prepared. The enemy's unity of command can be greatly reduced by using the principle of surprise. The rule of surprise, when employed correctly, leads to confusion and conflicting orders throughout the ranks of the enemy. When the enemy's command is caught off-guard by surprise, the rule of the offensive and mass-power are greatly enhanced in favor of the special ops church.

ABSOLUTE AND RELATIVE SUPERIORITY

The special ops church must realize that absolute superiority is not realistically attainable everywhere on the battlefield until the enemy surrenders unconditionally. Absolute superiority must be replaced frequently by relative superiority somewhere on the battlefield.

Similarly, every apostolic leader must determine his sphere of influence and not wander beyond that arena. Leaders possessed by controlling spirits usually want absolute superiority over not only their sphere of influence, but also everything they can see, touch, or feel. This flaw in a leader can send him to an early grave because of self-induced stress. We can find our best counsel as special ops Christians from the examples of absolute and relative superiority found in the strategic plan associated with the reign of Christ and the discipling of nations.

Absolute superiority, in the spiritual sense, means total dominion over Christ's enemies. A good example of this can be found in the following scriptures.

> After that comes the end (the completion), when He delivers over the kingdom to God the Father after rendering inoperative and abolishing every [other] rule and every authority and power.
>
> —1 CORINTHIANS 15:24, AMP

> Then the eleven disciples went away into Galilee, into a mountain where Jesus had appointed them. And when they saw him, they worshipped him: but some doubted. And Jesus came and spake to them, saying, All power is given unto me in heaven and in earth.
>
> —MATTHEW 28:16

Relative superiority, in the spiritual sense, means partial dominion— having the upper hand, short of total dominion—over all of Christ's enemies. A good example of this can be found in the following scripture.[3]

> The Lord (God) says to My Lord (the Messiah), Sit at My right hand, until I make Your adversaries Your footstool.
>
> —PSALM 110:1, AMP

> For [Christ] must be King and reign until He has put all [His] enemies under His feet.
>
> —1 CORINTHIANS 15:25

By just sitting, the Lord is not trying to solve all the ills of the world, thus demonstrating that relative superiority is an effective tactic at times.

Remember that absolute superiority everywhere is unattainable in a special ops church's sphere of influence. Absolute superiority must frequently be replaced with relative superiority in the sphere of influence. It is a lie from the enemy that you are losing the war if you do not have superiority over the entire battlefield.

In 2 Corinthians the apostle Paul speaks of his sphere of influence, emphasizing that he does not go beyond or overreach that sphere. Achieving relative superiority somewhere in your sphere of influence is the main objective of any strategic or tactical objective. Relative superiority is the intermediate objective that the apostolic command of the special ops church should try to accomplish.

Spiritual Post-Traumatic Stress Disorder

Violation of the principles of absolute superiority and relative superiority on the battlefield can lead to what I call spiritual post-traumatic stress disorder (SPTSD) in the best and highest-ranking special ops Christians. The symptoms of SPTSD and post-traumatic stress disorder (PTSD) are almost identical. In the military veterans' community, post-traumatic stress disorder is called shell shock, survivor guilt syndrome, and forgotten warrior syndrome. The symptoms include:

- bitterness
- anger
- anxiety
- depression
- loneliness
- alienation
- sleeplessness
- flashbacks to combat (In SPTSD, these could manifest as flashbacks to severe spiritual warfare.)
- suicidal feelings
- drug and alcohol dependence
- porn and sexual addiction

It has been diagnosed as a psychiatric disorder than can manifest years after the witnessing of life-threatening events, natural disasters, terrorist incidents, serious accidents, or violent personal assaults.[4] In like manner, spiritual warfare can create events that are life-threatening. Natural disasters can oppress the believer with fear and a sense of loss. Serious accidents can leave believers and non-believers with fear and anxiety. Violent personal assaults, whether physical, spiritual, or emotional, can leave even the toughest special ops Christians traumatized.

Nothing wounds or kills the spirit of a warrior like dishonor. You can only quench the spirit of a true warrior by one method, and that is by dishonoring him. I have heard Christians call it the dark night of the soul, a term coined by the sixteenth-century poet Saint John of the Cross. A lack of understanding by the church community concerning SPTSD can bring much dishonor on a Christian warrior. Many Christian ministers feel they can live above the stress of their calling. They fear exposing any emotional or spiritual weakness because they know corporate climbers in the church world will use it against them. Those suffering from SPTSD are often riddled with guilt over their supposed lack of faith.

Violation of the principles of absolute superiority and relevant superiority on the battle field can directly lead to SPTSD for the special ops Christian in command and for those following him or her. Absolute superiority can needlessly cost you numerous causalities that could have been avoided with the right approach to the battle. Zeal mixed with immaturity or a messianic complex can be costly.

During my Vietnam combat experience, I adopted the principle that my special ops team would always live to fight another day. In the movie *Patton*, the World War II legend said it something like this: "Men, I don't want you laying down your life for your country; I want you to make the enemy lay down his life for his country."[5] I know the great responsibility a military officer caries concerning the lives of his men in combat. I never asked one of my men in combat to do something I wouldn't do myself. I also could not become reckless in my decisions by exposing my team to unnecessary emotional or physical trauma.

I notice some leaders in the body of Christ are prone to trying to achieve absolute superiority on the battlefield. This new generation of special ops Christians is too valuable to waste. We should act wisely when deploying them to the nations. We should not impart a martyr complex into these precious kids. We should serve them as wise generals who can send them into battle and extract them as safely as possible from the battle. This young generation is already seeing the horrible suffering and carnage of civil war on several continents. We must be ready to heal the spiritual, emotional, and physical wounds this young generation is suffering for the cause of Jesus Christ. We must be ready to honor their service, because dishonor destroys the spirit of the warrior. My generation has been given a great responsibility by God to get it right in helping this next generation further usher in the kingdom of God.

Relative superiority on the battlefield is a wise approach to managing the war. Economy of force is one of the nine principles of war that works well with relative superiority. Leaders must refrain from throwing every resource into the battle. Manpower, finances, and prayer should be measured out in a way that allows the special ops church to answer the enemy's counterattack.

Over the years, my wife Barbara and I have had the assignment to try and restore missionary families that are suffering from SPTSD from too many years on the battlefield. Often these volunteer missionaries suffer from the same symptoms our all-volunteer military suffers from. It is reported that about 30 percent of our veterans from battlefields in Afghanistan and Iraq are suffering from some degree of PTSD. I have worked with SPTSD in missionaries and PTSD in military veterans. I am convinced that the stress of both these callings can break down individuals, families, and the institutions these volunteers represent.

I have found some of the most SPTSD-damaged believers are former pastors and key church workers. Often these brothers and sisters had their honor assaulted by evil forces inside the institution they served. It is a mandate of the special ops church to restore these valuable individuals and get them back in service, if possible. We need retreat centers for valid wounded warriors to recover. It is the responsibility of the special ops to find these retreat centers and get the wounded warrior there for healing. Some of these centers already exist and are staffed.

Those believers who feel they are suffering from spiritual post-traumatic stress disorder should take the following action:

- Find a good inner-healing program that is experienced and confidential.
- Seek a deliverance ministry that is experienced and confidential.
- Slow down your pace of life and spend time soaking in anointed worship.
- Identify areas of your life that cause SPTSD and eliminate or modify them.
- Find a good retreat center and visit it frequently until your healing manifests.
- Begin to use the nine principles of war as guides to judgment for decisions.
- Read and speak the promises of healing found in the Word of God.

The principle of war known as maneuver could dramatically change the stress levels of special ops Christians who are called to the nations. Maneuver is the mobility and flexibility of personnel in an effort to achieve your objective. It exploits successes, preserves freedom of action, and reduces vulnerability to enemy advances. Maneuvering can position personnel in such a way the enemy is at a relative disadvantage. It saves manpower and materials but requires flexibility in organization, administrative support, command, and control. The special ops church must be flexible. Leaving missionaries on the field long-term is generally part of an old paradigm. Maneuver is the antithesis of permanence and implies avoidance of stereotyped patterns of operation. By nature, special ops Christians usually want to launch into new, anointed ways to minister. Special ops Christians must live to fight another day, so let's fight smart.

SECURITY

Many military war fighters identify the rule of security as an element of surprise. The rule of security emphasizes the protection of everything vital to the accomplishment of your objectives. In the special ops church this begins and ends with the special ops Christian. Proverbs 4:20–27 is the passage of Scripture that most closely relates to the rule of security.

> My son, attend to my words; incline thine ear unto my sayings. Let them not depart from thine eyes; keep them in the midst of thine heart. For they are life unto those that find them, and health to all their flesh. Keep thy heart with all diligence; for out of it are the issues of life. Put away from thee a froward mouth, and perverse lips put far from thee. Let thine eyes look right on, and let thine eyelids look straight before thee. Ponder the path of thy feet, and let all thy ways be established. Turn not to the right hand nor to the left: remove thy foot from evil.

In spiritual warfare, the rule of security is birthed in the heart of the special ops Christian and has a tremendous impact on the church. Out of the heart come the issues of life. When the special ops Christian opens his mouth at the wrong time with the wrong words, it can aid and abet the enemy. Words can wound, uncover, and create either good or evil, as we will learn in the chapter on the weapon.

Security is essential to the preservation of combat power. Unbelief is a major enemy to preserving power in the life of a special ops Christian. Proverbs 4:24 warns us to "put away...a froward mouth, and perverse lips." A froward mouth is an unbelieving mouth. Unbelief can be devastating to the preservation of power in general. It is like a cracked vase that leaks water, so vital to the preservation of the flowers in it.

Diligence is the operative word for the special ops Christian who wants security to work in a steady, consistent effort toward the accomplishment of the tactical objectives being undertaken. Security through guarding the heart must be done with much diligence. Proverbs 4:23 states:

> Keep thy heart with all diligence; for out of it are the issues of life.

Security is achieved by measures taken in the area of words, which begin within the heart of the special ops Christian. This will prevent surprise, preserve freedom of action, and deny the enemy information. Proverbs 4:1 states:

> Hear, My sons, the instruction of a father, and pay attention in order to gain and to know intelligent discernment, comprehension, and interpretation [of spiritual matters]. (AMP)

The ability to intelligently discern, comprehend, and interpret spiritual matters can stop security breaches in the heart before the tongue releases them. Jesus calls us friends and promises to share all secrets with us:

> I do not call you servants (slaves) any longer, for the servant does not know what his master is doing (working out). But I have called you My friends, because I have made known to you everything that I have heard from My Father. [I have revealed to you everything that I have learned from Him].
>
> —JOHN 15:15, AMP

Since risk is inherent in war, application of the principle of security does not imply undue caution and the avoidance of calculated risk in the life of the special ops Christian. The promise of the Lord in Proverbs 4:18 should erase all undue caution and release us in faith concerning calculated risk:

But the path of the just is as a shining light, that shineth more and more unto the perfect day.

The rule of surprise is used in tandem with the rule of security. Surprise is offensive action that uses mass-power, economy of force, and maneuver to prevent security from becoming a permanent defensive posture. Security should never promote a defensive posture. Through surprise, the rule of security is enhanced by bold seizure and retention of initiative, which denies the enemy the opportunity to interfere with the tactical objective of the special ops church.[6]

Proverbs 28:1 reinforces this boldness, stating:

The wicked flee when no man pursueth: but the righteous are as bold as a lion.

The defensive position is a resting posture. God's people are as bold as lions and do great exploits.

Security within the heart of the apostolic leader of a special ops church will not guarantee the success of this rule of conduct. Even security in the hearts of other leaders will not ensure the success of this rule of conduct. As has been stated before, the strength of the special ops church is the special ops Christian, and the strength of the special ops Christian is the special ops church. The heart of each special ops Christian must be pure or security will break down. When security breaks down it causes a domino effect, and other principles, such as unity of command, the objective, and the offensive, begin to fail. No matter how strong the apostolic leadership, special ops churches can be destroyed by internal security failures in the heart of special ops Christians.

SIMPLICITY

The organization of plans as well as communication of orders in a simple, clear, and concise manner

To a large degree, simplicity enhances all the other principles of war.

Simplicity is a crucial element of any battle plan. In his book *On War*, Clausewitz states, "In war everything looks simple; the knowledge required does not look remarkable, the strategic options are so obvious that by comparison the simplest problem of higher mathematics has an impressive scientific dignity." He goes on the say, "The military machine the army and everything related to it is basically very simple and therefore seems easy to manage…In theory it sounds reasonable enough…In fact, it is different, and every fault and exaggeration of the theory is instantly exposed in war."[7]

When encountered, spiritual warfare tends to expose every major weakness in a church. In an effort to overcome this, a special ops church needs to apply the rule of simplicity to its organization, methods, and means. This will provide an atmosphere of orderliness in operations related to its sphere of influence. Direct, simple plans and clear, concise orders minimize misunderstanding and confusion among special ops Christians. The simplest plan is preferred if the other rules of conduct have been obeyed.

The plan is something that cannot be ignored. The building blocks of the plan are as follows:

- the grand strategic objective of Jesus Christ
- the mission of the special ops church
- the vision of the special ops church
- the code of conduct
- the rules of conduct—the nine principles of war
- strategic and tactical goals and objectives

By way of review, the grand strategic objective of Jesus Christ is the discipling of nations, as stated in Matthew 28:18–20. The mission of the special ops church states why it exists. The vision of the special ops church states where it is headed. The code of conduct is the guide for behavior on the journey toward the vision while walking out the plan. The rules of conduct, which are essentially the nine principles of war, are guides to judgment while on the journey toward the vision. Strategic and tactical goals and objectives help us bridge the gap between the present and the future as defined in the vision.

The strategic objective, united with tactical goals and operations in a good plan, will guide the special ops church for the next ten to twenty years. Tactical goals and operations alone in a good plan will guide the special ops church for no longer than one year or until the next budget submission. Prior to drafting either the strategic objective or tactical operations for a special ops church, leadership must agree on the grand strategic objective of Jesus Christ and the mission, vision, code of conduct, and rules of conduct for a special ops church.

CHAPTER 8

THE WEAPON OF CHOICE

During a direct confrontation with the enemy, nothing could be worse than to have your weapon malfunction in combat. A battle I was in on Hill 551 in Vietnam taught me the importance of my weapon functioning properly. Seconds after diving into the bomb crater with the rest of our eight-man recon team, an enemy soldier popped up not twenty-five feet away from me. I thrust my M-16 weapon at him and pulled the trigger in a quick kill maneuver we had learned in training. Click, my weapon had jammed. I felt limp and helpless as I tried to clear the chamber manually. Out of the corner of my eye, I saw the muzzle of another M-16 come up over my right shoulder. My ears rang as a shot from the weapon went off next to my ear. The enemy soldier fell backward and slumped out of my line of sight. Ric Miller had just picked off the enemy with a single shot over my shoulder. My ears still ringing, I pulled an M-79 grenade launcher off my shoulder. I shoved a high-explosive round into the chamber and fired the first blast into the enemy's position. I fired over one hundred devastating high-explosive rounds over the next three-and-one-half-hour battle. Toward the end of the battle, I grabbed my M-16 and used it successfully as we fought our way back to an extraction helicopter. Anyone who knows weapons knows the problem with my M-16 was a faulty gas system that didn't eject the spent round casing. I had successfully fired the weapon as I headed to the crater, but then another malfunction occurred. I never trusted that weapon again. Within weeks I purchased a Swedish K, 9mm automatic weapon with blowback action that prevented malfunctions like I had experienced on Hill 551.[1]

Without his weapon functioning properly, the Special Ops Christian is dead meat.

THE BIBLE HAS A DEFINITE MILITARY THEME

Exodus 15:3 declares, "God is a Man of War" (AMP). Although the Old Testament is rich in the military theme with warriors such as David, Deborah, Sampson, and Gideon, we also pick up this theme in the New Testament.

Jesus paid a soldier a gracious complement in Matthew 8:8–10: "But the centurion replied to Him, Lord, I am not worthy or fit to have You come under my roof; but only speak the word, and my servant boy will be cured. For I also am a man subject to authority, with soldiers subject to me. And I say to one, Go, and he goes; and to another, Come, and he comes; and to my slave, Do this, and he does it. When Jesus heard him, He marveled and said to those who followed Him [who adhered steadfastly to Him, conforming to His example in living and, if need be, in dying also], I tell you truly, I have not found so much faith as this with anyone, even in Israel" (AMP).

The soldier properly discerned the power of the spoken word. He told Jesus that He need only speak the word and the boy would be healed (v. 8). Jesus replied, "I tell you truly, I have not found so much faith as this with anyone, even in Israel" (v. 10). Jesus seemed to be impressed with how the soldier discerned the spiritual authority of the spoken word through the natural authority of his military experience.

It is time for Christians to understand and heed the military model in the Bible. Special ops Christians must have the discipline and understanding of a good natural soldier if they are to complete their mission.

The weapon of choice for the special ops church is the Word of God, like the centurion soldier recognized in Jesus. The weapon is not physical but mighty to the pulling down of strongholds (2 Cor. 10:4). As special ops Christians we do not use mere human weapons. Instead, according to 2 Corinthians 10:5, "[We] refute arguments and theories and reasonings and every proud and lofty thing that sets itself up against the [true] knowledge of God; and we lead every thought captive into the obedience of Christ (the Messiah, the Anointed One)" (AMP).

THE SPECIAL OPS WEAPON IS THE WORD OF GOD

During spiritual warfare, there are many practical steps taken by members of a special ops church. Praise, of course, is a mighty weapon, and so is prayer. Both can be coupled with the Word of God to create a weapon of mass destruction in the spiritual realm. I highly recommend Chuck Pierce and John Dickson's book on praise, called *The Worship Warrior*.

My primary goal in this chapter is to teach special ops Christians how to use God's Word as a weapon. A soldier who wages war in the natural must know how to assemble his weapon. The same principle applies to the special ops Christian and the weapon he uses to wage warfare in a spiritual battle. The special ops Christian must know how the Word of God is assembled to create an ultimate spiritual weapon. It starts with faith.

The Special Ops Christian and church must live by faith.

> Behold his soul which is lifted up is not upright in him: but the just shall live by his faith.
>
> —HABAKKUK 2:4

> For therein is the righteousness of God revealed from faith to faith: as it is written, The just shall live by faith.
>
> —ROMANS 1:17

But that no man is justified by the law in the sight of God, it is evident: for, The just shall live by faith.

—Galatians 3:11

Now the just shall live by faith: but if any man draw back, my soul shall have no pleasure in him.

—Hebrews 10:38

We must answer the question, What is faith and how does the special ops Christian live by it?

Now faith is the substance of things hoped for, the evidence of things not seen.

—Hebrews 11:1

So faith is the substance of all things. Without faith-substance, it is impossible to create the spiritual weapon needed to wage warfare in a spiritual war. Faith is the substance of what? It is the substance of things hoped for, or desired. Faith is the substance of a Christian's hope in successfully serving the Lord and accomplishing the mission. Beyond hope, faith is also evidence. The Amplified Bible says, "Now faith is the assurance (the confirmation, the title deed) of things [we] hope for, being the proof of things [we] do not see and the conviction of their reality [faith perceiving as real fact what is not revealed to the senses]" (Heb. 11:1).

God made all things with the Word. God had to use faith when he made all things. God's material for His spiritual weapon is faith.

Our next question must be, How did God make all things by faith? The following scriptures demonstrate the how God's words were like creative spiritual bullets during Creation.

- Genesis 1:3—"God said…and there was."
- Genesis 1:6–7—"God said…and it was so."
- Genesis 1:9—"God said…and it was so."
- Genesis 1:11—"God said…and it was so."

- Genesis 1:14–15—"God said... and it was so."
- Genesis 1:20—"God said"
- Genesis 1:24—"God said... and it was so."
- Genesis 1:26—"God said"
- Genesis 1:29–30—"God said... and it was so.

Finally, Genesis 1:31 tells us that "God saw every thing that he had made." God was saying to make things. If God was saying to make things, we must also create things by faith professed through our speech. Our weapon as special ops Christians is saying words that are filled with faith-substance to create a spiritual weapon that allows us to protect and serve in the kingdom of God.

ASSEMBLING AND FIRING THE SPECIAL OPS WEAPON

The special ops Christian can envision his weapon resembling the following:

1. His mouth as the barrel of the weapon.

2. His heart is where the ammunition (God's Word) is stored like an ammo magazine.

3. His tongue is the trigger that releases the Word of God out of the ammo magazine of his heart through the barrel of his mouth and onto the target. The Word can bless what is godly and either change or destroy what is ungodly.[2]

Firing our weapon is as simple as opening our mouths and firing or speaking the Word of God with our tongues. The power of the weapon is connected to our understanding concerning faith, the kingdom of God, and the anointing of God. The more we understand and walk in these three truths, the more powerful our weapon becomes. Abandoning faith, operating outside the laws of the kingdom of God, and failing to discern the authority of your anointing will dissipate the power of your spiritual weapon. Let's break down the weapon:

- The special ops Christian lives by faith.
- The kingdom of God is the supernatural system that dictates how God does things in our lives.
- The anointing or power of the Holy Spirit is the issue or force of life that comes out of your heart. The anointing determines the power of the Word of God being released out of your mouth (the barrel) from (the ammunition magazine of) your heart through using your tongue (as the trigger).
- Remember that the Word must have the Holy Spirit's anointing or it turns into legalism. It is the Word and the Spirit that give life.

PRACTICAL USE AND UNDERSTANDING OF THE WEAPON

The following is an example of using the weapon of the Word concerning a special ops Christian's need for provision.

Therefore take no thought, saying, What shall we eat? or, What shall we drink? or, Wherewithal shall we be clothed? (For after all these things do the Gentiles seek:) For our heavenly Father knoweth that ye have need of all these things. But seek ye first the kingdom of God, and his righteousness; and all these things shall be added unto you.

—MATTHEW 6:31–33

Your heavenly Father knows all about your needs. Philipians 4:19 says God has the supply for our every need.

Matthew 6:33 in the Amplified Bible expresses the kingdom of God this way: "But seek (aim at and strive after) first of all His kingdom and His righteousness (*His way of doing and being right*), and then all these things taken together will be given you besides" (emphasis added). The question for the special ops Christian and church should be, What is God's way of doing things? The answer may be found in Genesis 8:22.

> While the earth remaineth, seedtime and harvest, and cold and heat, and summer and winter, and day and night shall not cease.

Do cold and heat still remain? The answer is yes. Do summer and winter still remain? The answer is yes. Do day and night still remain? The answer is yes. Then seedtime and harvest must still remain.

A special ops Christian and church must know that God's way of doing things is through seedtime and harvest.

> And God said, Let us make man in our image, after our likeness: and let them have dominion.
>
> —GENESIS 1:26

> And God said, See, I have given you every plant yielding seed that is on the face of all the land and every tree with seed in its fruit; you shall have them for food.
>
> —GENESIS 1:29, AMP

God gave Christians and the church dominion and seed.

> And Jesus said, So is the Kingdom of God, as if a man should cast seed into the ground; And should sleep, and rise night and day, and the seed should spring and grow up, he knoweth not how. For the earth bringeth forth fruit of herself; first the blade, then the ear, after that the full corn in the ear. But when the fruit is brought forth, immediately he putteth in the sickle, because the harvest is come. And he said, Whereunto shall we liken the kingdom of God? or with what comparison shall we compare it? It is like a grain of mustard seed, which, when it is sown in the earth, is less than all the seeds that be in the earth: But when it is

sown, it groweth up, and becometh greater than all herbs, and shooteth out great branches; so that the fowls of the air may lodge under the shadow of it.

—MARK 4:26–32

Once again we see in the kingdom of God there is like seedtime and harvest. The seed goes through three steps, or a progression, over time:

1. the blade
2. the ear or processing the seed
3. the full ear of corn (harvest time)

How do faith, the kingdom of God, and the anointing work together, forming a weapon for the special ops Christian?

Matthew 17:20 says, "If ye have faith as a grain of mustard seed...nothing shall be impossible to you." The question is not if you have faith but how are you treating your faith? You must plant your seed.

And the apostles said unto the Lord, Increase our faith. And the Lord said, If ye had faith as a grain of mustard seed, ye might say unto this sycamine tree, Be thou plucked up by the root, and be thou planted in the sea; and it should obey you.

—LUKE 17:5–6

Jesus didn't say that the apostles needed more faith. The question, once again, was one of how they were treating their faith. Were they treating it like a seed with good soil, water, weeding, and other, proper care?

What does the seed symbolize in relationship to the weapon of the special ops Christian?

The seed is the incorruptible Word of God, the ammunition of the special ops Christian's weapon.

The Weapon of Choice

Being born again, not of corruptible seed, but of incorruptible, by the Word of God, which liveth and abideth for
ever.

—1 Peter 1:23

It is impossible for God to lie because His words, which are spiritual
containers, have enough faith-substance in them that they bring into
existence the situation He speaks. God creates by the faith-filled words
spoken out of His mouth. This weapon is a creative force that has the
power to change situations and protect us from the powers of darkness
that are trying to destroy us. This is how the special ops Christian and
church make things by faith.

In the beginning was the Word, and the Word was with
God, and the Word was God.

—John 1:1

God makes the Word equal with Himself. In fact, God and His
Word are one. If God began with the Word, then we as special ops
Christians must start with the Word also.

What do God and His Word have in common?
Faith is ammunition in the weapon of a Special Ops Christians. The
same faith that is in the heart of God is the same faith that is the Word
of God. That deserves to be restated: the same faith that abides in God
abides in His Word. The same material, the same faith-substance, in
God is in His Word.

**The Word of God equals faith. You can substitute *the Word* for
faith. *Word* and *faith* are interchangeable terms.**
To live by faith is to live by the Word. Concerning faith, Hebrews
11:1 says, "Now faith is the assurance (the confirmation, the title deed)
of things [we] hope for" (AMP). Now exchange the *Word* for *faith*, and
it says, "Now *the Word* is the assurance (confirmation, the title deed)
of things [we] hope for." Thus, an absence of the Word means there

is no assurance, confirmation, or title deed of things hoped for. The Word is our confirmation slip.

Now read Hebrews 11:3–8 and exchange *the Word* with *faith*:

> Through *the Word* we understand that the worlds were framed by the *faith* of God, so that things which are seen were not made of things which do appear. By *the Word* Abel offered unto God a more excellent sacrifice than Cain, by which he obtained witness that he was righteous, God testifying of his gifts: and by it he being dead yet speaketh. By *the Word* Enoch was translated that he should not see death; and was not found, because God had translated him: for before his translation he had this testimony, that he pleased God. But without *the Word* it is impossible to please him: for he that cometh to God must believe that he is, and that he is a rewarder of them that diligently seek Him.

The following scriptures provide yet further evidence that *faith* and *the Word* may be used synonymously.

The just shall live by his faith [the Word].
—HABAKKUK 2:4

The just shall live by faith [the Word].
—ROMANS 1:17

The just shall live by faith [the Word].
—HEBREWS 10:38

The just shall live by faith [the Word].
—GALATIANS 3:11

The Word of God and faith are a weapon in the hands of the special ops Christian and the special ops church.

> My son, attend to my words; incline thine ear unto my sayings. Let them not depart from thine eyes; keep them in the midst of thine heart. For they are life unto those that find them, and health to all their flesh. Keep thy heart with all diligence; for out of it are the issues of life. Put away from thee a forward mouth, and perverse lips put far from thee.
>
> —PROVERBS 4:20–24

The power in the weapon of a special ops Christian depends on what he feeds his eyes, ears, and mouth, because it goes to his heart. In turn, his anointing comes from his heart, or spirit. For this reason, the power of the weapon of the special ops Christian and the special ops church is proportionate to the anointing that flows from the hearts of disciples.

The special ops Christian and the special ops church must use their mantle of authority and wield the weapon of the Word with impunity against the kingdom of darkness. The following are some examples of using the weapon:

- For illness, pray: "By the stripes of Jesus Christ I was healed." (See 1 Peter 2:24.)
- For more finances, pray: "There is no lack, for my God shall supply all of my needs according to His riches by glory in Christ Jesus my Lord." (See Philippians 4:19.)
- For defeating fear, pray: "The fear of man will put a noose around your neck, and God hasn't given me a spirit of fear, but one of love, power, and a disciplined mind." (See 2 Timothy 1:7, AMP.)

In summary, I would like to encourage the apostolic leadership of the special ops church to secure a solid unity of command. Next, I would suggest that the objective of the church be clearly stated. The principle of the offensive flows out of unity of command and the objective. The principles of mass-power, economy of force, and maneuver flow out of the offensive, and security, surprise, and simplicity flow out of the three phases of the offensive. Remember, the special ops Christian should be applying the nine principles of war to his own life. This will make for a successful special ops church.

CHAPTER 9

THE SPECIAL OPS WOMAN

WHEN IT COMES to the subject of special ops women and the special ops church, I really must defer to my wife Barbara's book on the subject. In 1971, Barbara and I joined the Kathryn Kulhman Ministry. This was our first experience with women in ministry, and it was wonderful. Kathryn was a beautiful example of a powerful woman working in ministry with powerful men following her lead and covering her spiritually.

I was being mentored by one of these men in the 1970s and saw the fasting and prayer he did for Kuhlman's healing ministry. He was one of her head ushers and confidants. Through this man's example, I learned how to pray for Barbara while she was ministering. His name was Perry Ratekin and he and his wife, Ruth, led over thirty thousand marines to the Lord during the Vietnam War. He had all their names written in thick albums. There were records that accounted for 450 of these marines who had received the baptism in the Holy Spirit. There were sixty major miracles reported by marines who had returned to the base healed of broken bones and with their casts removed. Every Saturday night for nearly twenty years he and Ruth opened the doors to the Christian Services Men's Center in Oceanside, California. The main gate was not far from Camp Pendleton Marine Corps Base. I learned how Perry worked as a partner with his wife in the ministry. I also saw how he worked with a powerful woman like Kathryn Kuhlman. Men who despise women in ministry are dinosaurs who should not be taken seriously.

Through nearly forty years of ministry God has taught me a great deal about the value of women in ministry. I had a ringside seat during the flawed Shepherding Movement of the 1970s and 1980s, which sentenced women to obey their husbands and stay out of any significant ministry. The Shepherding Movement was a pathetic attempt by a bunch of insecure and unqualified men to somehow organize the kingdom of God into a male-controlled nation. It was not much different than the Taliban's approach to women in Afghanistan. The burqas worn by the women who got trapped in the Shepherding Movement were unseen spiritual veils that quenched their spirits and destroyed their personalities. The only redeeming thing about spending ten years trying to make the Shepherding Movement work in my life is the ability to now use it as an example of what not to do to women. The Shepherding Movement was kind of a multi-level marketing approach to kingdom building in which those who got in first—no matter if they had the anointing or not—were the most honored. Horrible men with little or no anointing grabbed the reigns of this movement and rode marriages and ministries into the ground.

Leadership in the Shepherding Movement, from the top to the bottom, was riddled with self-promoting bigots who were great at posturing themselves as apostles, prophets, evangelists, pastors, and teachers. Much of this posturing was at the expense of valid, young, anointed five-fold ministers, both male and female. Certain leaders of the Shepherding Movement made sure the anointed ministers got pushed down to the bottom of the food chain of ministry where there were no finances or ministry opportunities.

The leaders of the Shepherding Movement were always talking about emerging ministry. However, in ten years of observing the emerging principle, all I saw emerge were bigger homes, cars, and bank accounts for the leaders. Why, you ask, did it take ten years for me to figure this out? Probably so that I could write about it with apostolic authority and to protect the special ops church, and especially our special ops women, from falling into the Shepherding Movement's slimy pit. I have much disdain for what those men did and continue to try to do with women in ministry.

Where did the Shepherding Movement really go astray? The answer: authority. The Shepherding Movement went beyond the sphere of authority the apostle Paul was always cognizant of concerning his own ministry. Men who had no apostolic calling went about proclaiming their apostleship. Others fashioned themselves as prophets, scaring people with dark words supposedly from the Lord that were ridiculous and controlling. Valid teaching ministries, such as those of Ern Baxter and Derek Prince, were lured into the Shepherding snare in search of relationship and covering for their independent teaching ministries. Baxter and Prince were the first to sniff out injustices in the Shepherding Movement, and by the mid 1980s Baxter and Prince were distancing themselves from the movement.

Yes, these are tough words, but what the Lord is doing with women in this present move of the Holy Spirit must not be effected by a bunch of narrow-minded male cowards who rule with a Jezebel spirit. The Jezebel spirit has no particular gender. It can come through a man just as easily as it can come through a woman. The Shepherding Movement engendered Jezebel in men's spirits by over-emphasizing male authority. Anointed men and women caught up in the Shepherding Movement were high-visibility targets for the Jezebel spirit. Men intimidated by leaders were forced to get their wives to completely obey them. Untrained, undisciplined Shepherding Movement leaders ran roughshod over men, women, and children like Nazis. There is no way to sugarcoat this ungodly treatment of women. My wife, Barbara, and I have forgiven the sins of people in the Shepherding Movement, but we will never forget the lessons we learned while trapped in its web of deceit. Never again!

Many churches are guilty of having a chauvinistic attitude toward women in ministry. I have chosen the Shepherding Movement as the embodiment of female abuse because in many ways that movement merely mirrored the attitude of the church toward women in the last century. This is not only a new century; it is a new millennium, with a new anointing on women in the ministry of the Lord Jesus Christ.

What are some ministry qualifications of a special ops woman in a special ops church?

- The special ops woman hears the Lord's voice but does not claim to hear God on every issue and circumstance of her life or others'.
- The special ops woman is respectful of other ministers' authority, both men and women, and does not act as though she is the only one who hears from God.
- The special ops woman is a team minister who plays a role in the mission and vision of discipling the nations for Jesus Christ. She is not a lone ranger hopping from one continent to another unaccompanied by other ministers.
- The special ops woman is a person of holiness, prayer, and fellowship, not an island unto herself.
- The special ops woman can operate in any of the five-fold ministry offices of apostle, prophet, evangelist, pastor, or teacher but waits for the recognition of these gifts from other five-fold ministers in her special ops church.
- The special ops woman lives by and values the special ops code of conduct and rules of conduct while moving strategically in team ministry.

These qualifications for ministry could easily be applied to a man as well.

WOMEN HEAL WOMEN

Over the years, Barbara and I have met many women who have been deeply hurt by the church or male authority figures in their lives. It is sad when we recognize the pain in these Christian women's lives. We may often detect a recurring phrase in their conversation: "and God told me." Barbara and I call it the God-told-me syndrome. This kind of woman makes all her own decisions, both good and bad, validating them with the same cliché. These individuals usually need healing before they are really ready for ministry. We have run into obviously wounded women who go from church to church correcting the pastor. Often a Jezebel spirit will enter into the woman's pain and begin to further isolate her.

A special ops woman is not a wounded person striking back at the church for the injustices she has suffered. A special ops woman who is commissioned into ministry is healed of past hurts or on the way to healing her wounded soul and spirit. For those of us in ministry, wounds from the enemy can happen often. Inner healing and deliverance ministry is a wonderful way to keep us pure through forgiveness toward those who have hurt us. Women are especially at risk in the church because of their sensitivity to the Spirit and openness to brothers and sisters in the faith. Maintaining a woman's soul and spirit is necessary to keep her fit for special ops missions.

The day of the lone ranger, Rambo-type ministry is just about over. The stakes are too high and the risk too great not to work as team members in ministry. Team ministry is the safest place for women and men alike in this present move of the Holy Spirit. My wife, Barbara, chose two mature women to assist her in ministry while preparing for a conference held in the spring of 2004 for thousands of women in Soweto, South Africa. To serve and protect these women, I selected three men, including myself, to be in attendance.

Finally, I must add that women will heal other women in this new, worldwide move. Men need not be intimidated by the powerful anointing of the Holy Spirit among our sisters. Men need to join their hearts and spirits with the valid women's movement that is beginning to take place. Women will have the grace in every culture and nation to lay hands on wounded women and bring about deliverance and inner healing. It is time for real men to display confidence and security in their masculine role in the church and encourage this women's movement.

I highly recommend my wife's book, *The Special Ops Woman*, as a must-read for women who feel called to be a part of the special ops church. The book is full of powerful strategic information with a military component especially designed to help women get organized for ministry, marriage, and business.

NOTES

INTRODUCTION

1. Carl von Clausewitz, *On War* (New York, NY: Penguin Classics, 1982), 101.

2. Everett F. Harrison, ed., *Baker's Dictionary of Theology* (Grand Rapids, MA: Baker Book House, 1960), 309–314.

1—DEFINING SPECIAL OPS

1. W. E. Vine, *Vine's Expository Dictionary of New Testament Words* (Nashville, TN: Royal Publishers, Inc., 1952), 1058–1059.

2. Ibid., 1210.

3. Ibid., 1209.

2—THE SPECIAL OPS CHURCH

1. Vine, 75–76.

2. Harrison, 123–126.

3. Dr. Bill Peters, The Godly Warrior Series, 1998.

4. From FIRST FORCE RECON COMPANY BY DR. BILL PETERS, copyright (c) 1999 by Dr. Bill Peters, Forword (c) 1999 by Lt. General Ormond R. Simpson. Used by permission of Ivy Books, a division of Random House, Inc.

5. *Webster's Desk Dictionary* (New York, NY: Gramercy Books, 1992), s.v. "warrior."

6. Ibid., s.v. "coalition."

7. Peters, *First Force Recon Company/Sunrise at Midnight*, 128–130.

8. *Webster's Desk Dictionary*, s.v. "union."

3—MISSION, VALUES, AND GUIDING PRINCIPLES

1. *Webster's Desk Dictionary*, s.v. "mission."

2. Peters, *First Force Recon Company/Sunrise at Midnight*, 79–99.

3. *Webster's Desk Dictionary*, s.v. "integrity."

4. Peters, *First Force Recon Company/Sunrise at Midnight*, 113–117.

5. *Webster's Desk Dictionary*, s.v. "team."

6. Peters, *First Force Recon Company/Sunrise at Midnight*, 108–113.

7. *Webster's Desk Dictionary*, s.v. "principle."

8. Peters, The Godly Warrior Series, 1998.

9. Ibid.

4—UNITY OF COMMAND

1. Peters, *First Force Recon Company/Sunrise at Midnight*, 103–108.

2. Vine, 159.

3. Harrison, 57.

4. Naomi Dowdy, *Commissioning: The Process, Protocol, and Importance of Commissioning Modern-day Apostles* (Dallas, TX: Naomi Dowdy Ministries, 2006), 21.

5. Chuck D. Pierce, *Interpreting the Times* (Lake Mary, FL: Charisma House, 2008), 206.

5—THE OBJECTIVE

1. Harry G. Summers, *On Strategy* (Novato, CA: Presidio Press, 1982), 94.

2. *Webster's Desk Dictionary*, s.v. "objective."

3. Peters, The Godly Warrior Series, 1998.

4. Ibid.

5. Ibid.

6. Peters, *First Force Recon Company/Sunrise at Midnight*, 214.

7. Peters, The Godly Warrior Series, 1998.

6—THE THREE-PHASE OFFENSIVE

1. Peters, *First Force Recon Company/Sunrise at Midnight*, 153–163.

2. Peters, The Godly Warrior Series, 1998.

3. Ibid.

4. Ibid.

5. Ibid.

6. Peters, *First Force Recon Company/Sunrise at Midnight*, 158–163.

7. Peters, The Godly Warrior Series, 1998.

8. Peters, *First Force Recon Company/Sunrise at Midnight*, 159–163.

9. Army Field Manual 100-5, February 19, 1962, 46.

10. Baron Colmar von der Goltz, *The Conduct of War: A Brief Study of Its Most Important Principles and Forms* (Kansas City, MO: The Franklin Publishing Co., 1896), 100, 193.

11. Peters, The Godly Warrior Series, 1998.

7—SECURITY, SURPRISE, SIMPLICITY

1. Peters, *First Force Recon Company/Sunrise at Midnight*, 167–170.

2. Peters, The Godly Warrior Series, 1998.

3. Ibid.

4. Dr. James W. Ralph, M.D., "Post-Traumatic Stress Disorder," *Purple Heart Magazine*, 2006–2007, 32–33.

5. *Patton*, written by Francis Ford Coppola and Edmund H. North, Twentieth Century Fox-Film Corporation, 1970.

6. Peters, The Godly Warrior Series, 1998.

7. von Clausewitz, 330–335.

8—THE WEAPON OF CHOICE

1. Peters, The Godly Warrior Series, 1998.

2. Ibid.

TO CONTACT THE AUTHOR
www.specialopschurch.com